Harriet Scott

Henrietta

A Novel

Harriet Scott

Henrietta
A Novel

ISBN/EAN: 9783337026684

Printed in Europe, USA, Canada, Australia, Japan

Cover: Foto ©Thomas Meinert / pixelio.de

More available books at **www.hansebooks.com**

HENRIETTA

A NOVEL

BY HARRIET SCOTT

MINNEAPOLIS, MINN.:
1892.

TO

MISS GRACE LIVINGSTON

THIS WORK IS

RESPECTFULLY DEDICATED.

HENRIETTA.

CHAPTER I.

"No, I cannot say that I consider the picture at all handsome."

"What fault have you to find?" asked Mrs. Desmond, a little severely. "I am sure that my niece, Miss Dudley, has always been considered a most charming woman, and that, too, by persons capable of judging in such matters."

"Charming she may be, my dear madam, as charming goes. That is often the result of manner, of facial expression, perhaps, too, enhanced by the strength of coloring; things not to be presented in their full force by the skill of the artist, however deft his work may be."

"But where is the fault?" persisted the old lady. "I can see none," as she donned her gold-rimmed specticles, after carefully wiping them on her dainty handkerchief.

Charles Lennox passed her the portrait.

"Observe," he said, "that the brow is rather too low, the mouth too large, and the nose is—how shall I term it?"

"Too *retrousse*," suggested Anna Desmond, glancing slyly up from her work, with an arch smile.

7

"Too what?" said her mother with energy. "Please speak plain English in my presence, Miss, and leave French for Frenchified people. I know well enough what you both mean, though. You pretend to think that Henriette has just a very common turn-up nose like any vulgar German or Celt might have. I really thank you for the compliment given to my brother's daughter; but wait till you see her before any more compliments are passed."

The lady arose stiffly and replaced the picture in its setting, the irony of her speech seeming to cling to her movements. She was past sixty, but still retained much of a spirit of worldliness, and of the dignified pride for which she had always been noted.

Charles Lennox both saw and felt that he had wounded that pride by his two open criticism of her niece, and he heartily wished that he had not spoken so hastily and thoughtlessly; but he had committed himself. He only hoped that no officious busy-body would tell the young lady so soon expected of his preconceived notions of her beauty.

Of course he would meet her. The two families of Lennox and Desmond were too intimate for him to think otherwise; and, of course, like others of her sex, she must set a great store by her looks. All women did, or all, at least, that had come under his observation during the period of his twenty-six years; all but one, and upon that one the conversation now turned.

"Have you heard of Eldie's good fortune?" asked Mrs. Desmond, after a restrained pause.

"No, I have heard of nothing unusual coming to her, either good or ill, but I have not seen any of them for more than a week."

"Quite a time I should say for one who seems so devoted as you do in that direction."

Her language carried with it the least perceptible sneer, but Lennox carefully concealed any annoyance it might have given him under a careless exterior, as he answered indifferently, "yes, both I and my mother think a great deal of Eldie; she is a nice girl, refined and cultivated beyond her station, and withal a person of considerable artistic talent."

"That is where her luck comes in, as she has sold her last picture for the sum of one hundred dollars, a great deal, you know, for her to receive."

"It is, truly, and I am glad to hear of it, as it will give the poor child encouragement to pursue her work, and, beside, the family must need it badly. But who was the purchaser?"

Mrs. Desmond turned an inquiring look toward her daughters.

"Can you tell us, girls? I really have forgotten the name."

"I think it was a Mrs. De Boise, a person of means, living far out on the Lyndale road. She came in her carriage, paid for the picture after a close examination of it, and took it away with her."

"I have quite forgotten the subject of her latest work. Was it a marine?"

"No; it was a very simple picture, and not at all original in design. She took it from an old family portrait, that of an aristocatic looking boy of six years, sitting upon a flowery bank with an old chateau in the background."

"Of course the picture is French, and they claim it to be that of some one of their ancestors. The child certainly showed marks of good blood, but good blood, so called, often falls very low, indeed, when it so far forgets itself as to mingle with that of inferior races."

"For my part I did not see anything remarkable enough about it to induce this strange lady—who, it appears, saw it at the exposition—to hunt Eldie up and to make the purchase."

"Some one who believes in patronizing home merit, perhaps, and in that she is right, too," said, Lennox.

"Yes, or, perhaps, some charitably disposed person, who, having heard of the situation of the family, thought to help them by this means. I suppose that it is really a good thing enough that the girl has a turn for painting, as God seems, in most of cases, to fit the back to the burden; but under different circumstances, that is, in a better frame of fortune, I should deem a gift of that sort in a woman a drawback of a most decided cast. It is so apt to encourage and strengthen those far-reaching aspirations which more properly belong to the opposite sex. Now, I don't want my daughters to be anything but good, quiet women, with thoroughly domestic tendencies, good house-keepers, and, in due time, if fortune so will it, that they marry and be good wives to the men who shall choose them."

The girls, twins of sixteen, blushed at their mother's plain discourse.

They were rather tall for their age, with the slender rounded form usual to their time of life, with fair complexion, very light brown hair, irregular features, and each of them a pair of large expressionless blue eyes. Their general appearance was so nearly alike that strangers found a difficulty in telling them apart.

Modest, innocent looking girls enough, with every appearance of the simple mediocrity which would give their parent no anxiety on the score of talent of any kind that might lead them out of the circumscribed orbit to which she firmly believed all women of right belonged.

Lennox arose and stepped toward the open piano where the girls had been practicing their lessons in the early part of the evening, and, wishing to divert the attention of the little group into a different and more agreeable channel, he seated himself in front of it, and running his fingers lightly over the keys he dashed off into a lively waltz, which somewhat shocked Mrs. Desmond, as she had come very near to a solemn vow at the time the organ had been exchanged for a piano, that nothing but sacred music should come from it; the same as she had always been accustomed to, for the lady had been a most conscientious church member for thirty years and more, and, in consequence, somewhat severe in her ideas of worldly amusement.

But Lennox did not, perhaps, know this, or if he did, he ignored the fact and kept on after the waltz was finished, with other lively airs, and, indeed, so excellent was the execution, and so grandly Appolo-like his movements, that she was charmed in spite of herself. She sincerely admired this young man, at any rate, and as she had always a most overwhelming passion for match-making, had set her heart upon a union between her niece, Henrietta Dudley, so soon expected from her home in Pennsylvania to spend the season with her.

Hence her tolerance of his present liberty, and hence the sarcastic flings and disparaging remarks she had cast toward the young artist, Eldie Janneaux, for whom she feared he might be forming an attachment.

She was likewise well pleased with his mother, a most fine and well-bred woman, and, indeed, with all his relatives, some of whom occupied an elevated social position in St. Paul, and what prestige it would give her and hers to be connected with such people; besides, there was the prospect of quite a nice fortune to come to him some day, when his only surviving parent should depart this life.

She never for a moment thought of either of her own daughters in connection with this union of

families, for the reason that they were too young
by several years to think of marriage; and by the
time they would reach the proper age, this man,
with his fair admiration for women, his winning
manners and magnificent bearing, would, in all
probability, be a husband.

He requested the girls to sing a duet, a simple
composition in which he had heard them before,
and with their mother's consent their pieces of
work in Kensington were carefully laid aside, and
they complied with his request.

The song finished, Lennox arose to go, and after
shaking hands with Mrs. Desmond, by way of a
sort of apology, perhaps, for the unamiable feelings his words had stirred in her breast, he
politely bowed to the rest and left the house.

In the room, beside Mrs Desmond and the two
girls, there was another person, quietly sitting
back in the shadow formed by a frame of flower-
ing plants, as silent and unobtrusive during the
conversation with their visitor as the plants
themselves.

It was John Desmond, the girls' brother, who,
although saying little or nothing, had, like most
untalkative people, noted all that was said with
the most minute exactness.

"I declare," said Mrs. Desmond, looking out of
the south window, "if Charles isn't going down
to the Janneaux's to-night, late as it is."

"I guess he must be in love with Eldie, for certain," said Sarah, as she assisted her sister to close
the piano and arrange the scattered pieces of

music; "and you will be out, John." She cast a mischievous look at her brother as she spoke.

John tried to smile, but it was evident that his heart was too sad. Mrs. Desmond looked toward him with surprise. It was the first intimation she had received that her son, too, might be affected by the fair young girl artist.

The two girls went into the kitchen to see if Christine, the Swedish maid, had ironed their white aprons yet, leaving John and his mother alone.

"I didn't know, John, that you cared anything for Eldie. Is it true?"

The young man moved uneasily in his chair, and looked toward the floor. He did not like a question quite so pointed, but he resolved in his mind that he must make some sort of answer, and the truth seemed to him the best.

"Yes, mother, I do care quite a good deal for Eldie, more than any girl I have ever met, and would make her my wife, although I well know that her culture and refinement, to say nothing of natural ability, would be an unequal match with the coarser parts of a plain farmer like myself."

"You are right there, my son; she would just make no match for you at all. I guess I have traveled long enough through this world, and seen enough to know that such women as she is never can make housekeepers, and that is what you want—a good, sensible girl, who will know her place as a wife, have your interest always the first in her mind, who will make her home and

yours the center of her attention, instead of looking out into the world after fame and the admiration of the vulgar crowd. Then you know as well
as I what the neighborhood whisper is in regard
to Eldie's antecedents."

"Yes, I have heard something of it," he said, his
face now flushed with anger; "and sometimes
these silly neighborhood whispers are more dis-
astrous in their consequences than the most ter-
tific tornado or cyclone. These can only destroy
property and life, but the first can take away
honor and reputation, things which to all persons
should be dearer than life."

The young man had arisen during this outburst
of passion, and was now walking the floor at a
rapid pace, his hands clenched nervously behind
him.

"I," he said, "have never taken much account
of this report. But you must have, by the manner in which you spoke to Lennox to-night about
the mingling of bloods. I saw your drift, if he
did not, and must say that I thought it in exceedingly bad taste, inasmuch as it displayed a vindic-
tive spirit toward one who has never harmed
either you or yours."

"I am not so sure of that," she replied; "not if
she has stolen your heart by her wiles, my son.
But let me ask you one more question and I have
done for the present. It is this: In case the story
of Eldie's parentage be true—that is, should be
proved without a doubt—how, then, would you
stand in regard to the matter?"

John was more exasperated than ever at the idea of his mother speaking of Eldie using undue arts to win him. Turning to her squarely, he said : "I should stand then precisely as I do now, knowing that I love her dearer than my own life. I would marry her at any rate, good and pure as she is. No responsibility rests upon her for the blood of her ancestors. If it be true — which I very much doubt — you must admit that the Indian is a long way back, as neither Eldie nor her sister show the least trace of it."

"I don't know that they do, but you know that one cannot always tell from appearances in such matters, and there are those who pretend to see their lineage plainly enough in their features ; but I promised to say no more to you on the subject at present. You have made me an honest answer, and I must bear it, displeasing as it is to me and will also be, I am sure, to your father when he hears of it. Good night, now, my son," and she drew his head down for a kiss ; "don't let this interview disturb you, but go to bed and sleep at once."

He did neither.

There were other and more distracting thoughts in his mind than those engendered by his mother's words—the thoughts of jealous rivalry, awakening to him slowly but surely, by Charles Lennox's attentions toward the object of his love. Instead of retiring, he sat at the window of his chamber above, looking moodily out over the lake in front of him; a sheet of silver in the moon's rays set in

its dark border of sedge and rushes; a calm scene
with not a sound to disturb its quiet, except the
least perceptible wave of steam borne up on the
night breeze from the busy city.

An hour later he saw Lennox coming from the
direction of the Janneaux cottage along the smooth
drive which skirted the opposite side of the lake
and led up to his mother's grounds and residence.

He looked after him with a pang of bitter hatred,
the first he had ever felt of so decided a nature
toward him, or any other creature for that matter,
and wondered whether Eldie cared much for him
and his fine scholarly attainments so far beyond
his own plainer ones.

Below stairs in her bit of a chamber, his mother
also lay long awake, thinking over the sudden
revelation which had been made to her by her
dearly loved son—the only one left to her from
the hand of Death among five — the son whose
happiness lay very close to her heart; and who
now, it seemed to her, was in a fair way of marring that happiness for life by his strong love for
this girl, Eldie Janneaux, whose ways and disposition she never could think suitable for him, to
say nothing of the tales which had been circu-
lated around in the community about her having
an Indian ancestor back somewhere in the past.

Of course, that might not really injure the girl,
but there was the eternal law of heredity staring
her in the face, a law which might come turning
up, the good Lord only could tell for how many
generations after, with its hideous face.

She had read but recently of a marriage of that
sort where the effected party was entirely free, so
far as could be observed, of any taint; but the
children born of her had strongly marked features,
denoting their descent, and their characteristics
agreed with their looks. What happened in that
case might happen again. Could anything be
more horrible than for John to have children, her
grandchildren, running about with a penchant for
ornaments of feathers and for tomahawks!

Still, this part of the girl's history might have
no truth in it; might be, for aught she knew, an
idle report; yet it had certainly gained quite a
wide circulation in the suburban settlement
around them. To tell the truth, none had been
more instrumental in this circulation than Mrs.
Desmond herself, for the lady was a good deal
of a gossip, and really considered it no harm
to tell all she knew or heard about people, good
or ill.

She had not originated among a people who
held a better doctrine, and she had never taken
sufficient thought on the subject to create one of
her own.

To be sure, she once picked up a Roman Catholic prayer-book, left in her kitchen by an Irish
servant, and cursorily turning over its pages, saw
there recorded that it is as great a sin to tell an
injurious truth as it is to formulate or report a
noxious falsehood. She gave the reading but a
momentary consideration, coming as it did from
such a source.

To her the old Romish church meant the beast with the seven heads, which had received a deadly wound in one of them at the time of the reformation, and the modern Romish Church was the beast with the two horns, as bad as the old one, because it teaches that the first knew no error. This, according to an interpetation of a part of the version of John the Revelator, and could anything good come out of Nazareth?

At any rate, she did not like the idea of John's marrying Eldie, be the story true or false, and, if possible, she would prevent it.

If young Lennox saw fit to get himself and family into trouble by such an alliance, why, of course, that was his own lookout. She would much rather it were he than her son; so she made up her mind to relinquish all thoughts of having him for a husband for Hetty, but instead to do all in her power to encourage him in the way his present inclinations seemed somewhat trending.

CHAPTER II.

It was a festal day for William Clipper.

His name was a misname, for he was not the least bit like the craft of that name on ordinary occasions, but more like a heavily-laden freight ship as he moved about with the slow but measured tread of a man who never allowed anything to push him, nor cared to push anything himself to any great extent.

But he was unusually happy just now, for he had made a great haul of fish the day before, not in the little lake, but in a stream a few miles above where pickerel were in abundance. There was nothing in the lake but cat-fish and no one around there cared for them but his neighbors, the Jaax family.

He had just came up from the city, where he had made a good sale, and brought home to his bit of a shanty quite a number of luxuries; and, what pleased him still better, a recently published work on geology and a new microscope to take the place of his old one.

He was a singular man, this Clipper, and generally considered among his neighbors as a shiftless sort of creature, with no evil worth speaking about in his make up, but with a store of philosophical learning which might, if possessed by a man of more energy of character, have made him a factor of no weak power among them.

He was a bachelor of perhaps thirty-eight, living alone and doing his work generally himself, unless it might be an occasional overhauling of his small amount of household goods given by Mrs. Jaax, and for which he paid her either in fish or game, these two being his prinpcial means of support, eked out by a batch of muskrat hides to sell to the furrier.

He was always botonizing around during his very many spare hours, or picking up bits of shells and geological specimens for analyzation, always watching the habits of birds and insects, and his cabin of two rooms was a veritable museum of curosities; a place where the student of natural history might have well devoted much time in his favorite pursuit.

He was decided only on one point, and that was his aversion toward the general ambition of mankind to become rich; and on this account he was always at cross-cuts with his neighbor, Jaax, who held opposition views fully as strong.

Jaax had come from "faderland," as his wife affectionately called their old home, Germany, a number of years back, and by dint of hard work on the part of the whole family, accompanied by the most strenuous economy, he had managed in the time to buy a few acres of miserable sandy land running up above the head of the lake. Here he had lived for twelve years or more, and was now considered to be a man of means, with quite a bank deposit.

His surroundings, however, were just the same as when he first commenced farming, as he always styled his business, with the row of cattle pens and horse stables still running the length and around the ends of his long, one-story building.

"They keeps him warm," he used to say, when speaking of his place, giving a sly chuckle at the time, as if he considered the plan of infinite more wisdom than that of his neighbors, who were willing to sacrifice this good for the sake of health and cleanliness.

Jaax's wife and children pined and dwindled into the most beggared and distressed specimens of humanity imaginable, for want of pure air ; but Jaax himself was robust to an unusual degree, because he spent but little time in-doors, his hours being mostly occupied either in attending to his cattle or in tilling his poor soil, upon which, he declared, he had put enough of fertilizing matter to make it productive clear through to China, and China must have got the benefit, for his crops were always thin and poor, no matter how much attention he gave them. The fall drought invariably scorched it all, but yet, despite this drawback, the old German had waxed well-to-do, and so was happy.

Clipper disliked him exceedingly. He could not well help it, as the difference was as great between them as the proverbial one between water and oil, with a corresponding natural antipathy.

Jaax was always twitting him of his poverty whenever they met, or asking him why he didn't try to find some regular employment and take a wife. Then Clipper would answer in his quiet, unruffled way, that he knew of some who had better not have wives, by the way they treated them.

It was the most sarcastic thing he ever did say, though, for he was a mild-tempered man and could scarcely be induced by any provocation to say so much to any one else beside this old man, upon whom he looked with almost as much contempt as he would a pig which had managed by greedy scrambles among its kind to accumulate a larger amount of food for his own use than his fellows were possessed of. In the contest after wealth he recognized no animus whatever. Nothing but the dull plodding and wretched unrest of inferior minds, and both in theory and practice he relied literally on the doctrine of Christ upon the subject.

He believed in it because it was the teaching of Christ.

Either, he mused, Jesus of Nazareth was the son of God, and as such to be followed by those professing his name in the spirit of truth, or else he was not the son of God, but a deception and altogether different from what he thought of himself.

He hated the hypocrisy of the nominal Christian in professing to believe in the Messiah, and yet in their daily life going diametrically opposite to his creed, under the specious names of individualism, progress, enterprise and the like, all of them but that spirit of mamon worship, as he considered, so deprecated throughout the pages of the New Testament.

His neighbors, that is, the greater number, looked upon him as being eccentric, and his freely spoken belief but the offspring of his irregular thought. No one could convince them that material riches were not a very good thing, indeed, a little more to be sought after than either spiritual or intellectual wealth, or at least to be looked after first as a foundation, as it were, upon which to unite the two last.

But William Clipper was not so eccentric as supposed, not essentially and by nature so, but the physical and mental force called forth by other men who had entered the matrimonial lists early in life, and as a natural accompaniment, had brought a train of children into the world, had lain dormant with him.

He had been late in life to find the woman of his choice, and in this choice an oddity of character certainly appeared.

It was for this woman that he was fixing up a string of his finest fish, reserved from those he had taken to the market in the earlier part of the day, and he had also indulged in the outlay of a sum of money sufficient to pay for a clear-voiced canary in a neat cage, to carry along with them.

Arrayed in his best suit, drab in color and the least bit old fashioned in make, he was about to start out, when he was arrested in his design by the entrance of a handsome, well-grown boy of

eighteen or more, his friend and frequent companion, Robert Orme, a being quite as much a
peculiarity as himself in his own different way,
being something of a naturalist, but a good deal
more of a lover of astronomy and poetry.

He delighted in giving new and dignified names
to things in nature.

The bits of emerald pebbles along the lake he
called jasper; carnelian, chelcedony; the whitish
flower found on the hardy patches of the hoary
leaved everlasting he called an edelweise; the
common meadow lily was the lily of the field, of
scripture, he was sure.

In addition to this poetic instinct, he knew as
much of sidereal and planetary movements as
some professors of astronomy, figuratively carry-
ing his head in the sky, and if his feet touched
the earth it was not with the tread of ordinary
mortals.

It was vacation month with him, and he was
spending it mostly in rambling about with his rod
or gun, or else getting specimens for Clipper's
cabinet.

But he had come on an errand this evening.

It was to see whether his friend would go over
to Mrs. Desmond's and drive the carriage to the
city depot after her niece, who was to arrive by
the noon train.

The answer was affirmative, and young
Orme, seeing that his friend was about to go out,
withdrew at an early opportunity and returned to
the Desmonds, where he found an attraction in

the form of one of the twins, a school-boy passion,
but none the less entrancing.

He divined where his friend was going, as he
knew, along with all the people about, of Clipper's
rather one-sided courtship with Hannah Shaw,
spinster, of an age equalling his own within a few
weeks, a temperament so different from his that
people wondered at his persevering efforts for the
last two years to win her grace.   .

He had never really asked Hannah to marry him.
although he had often thrown out broad hints to
that end, but only to be met with the forceful
rebuff, which mostly nips an unwelcome advance
in the bud, but not in Clipper's case, at least, leaving it without power to, in time, renew its decol-
lated parts.

Hannah was a wonder in some respects.

She was the best housekeeper, undisputably, in
the community. No one ever thought of rivalling
her in that way, well knowing that their linen of
the household could never be kept in the same
immaculate whiteness, that their cooking and
baking could never attain to the same excellence,
nor their art of cleanliness reach to the same
height; and then her garden had in it the
best vegetables to be found, while the two
narrow beds on either side of the long path
leading up through her front yard, were filled
with the finest of flowers, both old and new in
variety.

She dearly loved flowers, and in this was the
only point that she and her lover agreed upon, the

only chord of real sympathy upon which their opposite natures seemed to harmonize.

Hannah was out weeding her flowers when Clipper came along.

"Good evening, Hannah," he said, as he entered the gate, with his fish and his canary.

She arose from her stooping posture and looked at him straight, her small and slender form immovable as a statue, her irregular features and sharp brown eyes expressing considerable wonder, not unmingled with scorn, as they rested upon the burden which he bore.

She was not a handsome woman, or had she ever been, and to an ordinary person the look she now wore would have rendered her almost repulsive. But Clipper was in love—the love which comes to middle life, and which some contend is stronger than that of early manhood, and so he saw nothing but what was fair in Hannah.

"What on earth are you bringing there, William Clipper? I hope it's nothing for me," was her first greeting, as she cast a scornful look at the innocent fish hanging by his side and the yellow bird sitting upon its perch.

"Yes, that is just what I have got, something for you, and I hope you will have the goodness to accept them, too. I've had an unusual streak of luck to-day; in fact, all week, for that matter, my business has been unusually good, so I made up my mind to bring you this canary from the city. He's a splendid singer, the seller said, and will add a great deal, I think, to the comfort of your home, or pleasure, rather, and I hope you will think so, too."

"Well, I don't know what to say. Of course I can't find it in my heart to hate a little bird like that, but I never told you that I wanted one, nor even hinted it, and I will tell you in plain words that I think you had better have laid out your bit of money in something more useful, for yourself I mean, and not to have thought of me or my home."

"Well, I do think a great deal about you, Hannah, and of your house, too, but only as the place is made fair and dear by your presence, and if you refuse to accept the bird, why, of course, I shall have to take it back and try to get my money, as I have not got the time now, in the busy season, to care for it. My business is too pressing for that."

"I don't wish to hear any nonsense this evening," said Hannah. "You've been hinting at your love for me, and coming up here so much with your presents of berries and fish until all the country is talking of it. They just have the impudence to say, that I, Hannah Shaw, who has conducted herself straightly for near on to forty years is about to marry you, a man who calls fishing a business; and, like all of your class, as poor as a church-mouse; yet still goes about prating of the sinfulness of accumulations in the way of money and property, when the truth of it is you are too shiftless and too deficient in the necessary energy to gather up anything for yourself."

Hannah was cross at some gossip which she had heard the day before, and when women of her description are cross they can, and mostly do, say a great deal.

Her sudden tirade somewhat astonished her lover, but he stood his ground well, determined not to be beaten out of the plan he had formed of putting the question of their union direct at this time.

He sat down the cage in the heart of a blue-flowered bush.

"There!" said Hannah, taking it off with a contemptous jerk, "you've about ruined my Jacob's ladder."

"Polmoniums, my dear, they're polmoniums; Jacob's ladder is a very common and old-fashioned name, and not at all botanical."

"Well, Jacob's ladder suits me, I'm not so learned, thank goodness for it too, if learning makes them all as shiftless as you are."

She started to straighten up the prostrate plant, and Clipper likewise stooped to assist her, for he was sorry at his carelessness as much as she.

Their hands came in contact.

It was the first time in all of his long and singular courtship that he had ever been so close to Hannah, and his frame felt a magnetic thrill.

"Hannah!"

"What is it, Mr. Awkward? Don't you see you have broken a limb there?"

"I never yet have asked you to marry me."

"No, nor you better not."

"That's just what I came up for to-night."

"It's my house and bit of income, I guess, that you are after."

"No, it's yourself, Hannah, your own dear self. I don't care a fig for your money, much or little be it, and indeed I should be glad to see it swept away from you by some accident, so that I might take you to my place and show you how I could and would work for you."

"Shiftless views again; I wonder how I could live in your miserable lodgings. I guess we would both be in a state of destitution soon enough."

Clipper looked annoyed, and he felt all that his looks implied, at the thought of being defeated on a point which he had intended to be most affecting."

"Oh, no!" he said; "I didn't really wish to bring you to poverty. I only mentioned it by way of illustration, to prove my devotion to you."

"There, now!" retorted the spinster, "at last you have as good as acknowledged that you would not care for me without my little bit of worldly goods. I always have thought that you had more of an eye to that than to me, in spite of your constant talk about riches."

"Why, Hannah, how can you so blame a man for what he is as guiltless of as honey is of vinegar?"

She smiled at his odd comparison in spite of herself, and asked him if he considered himself anything like honey.

"No," he said; "but I certainly consider you quite like a honey bee, with its sting always prepared for war."

"Well, then, keep away from me, and you won't feel its point, is all I have to say."

"Yes, but I won't keep away, until you have fairly and squarely answered my question."

"What question, Mr. Clipper?"

He looked at her in a puzzled sort of way. He forgot that he had not as yet asked her to marry him, but only suggested it.

"I guess we could get along," he said, not knowing what else to say to make things still more plain to her.

"I know I can get along," answered his tormentor, "up to my house, but if a man of your queer way expects to get along, why, he had better not wait till the woods grow too dark. Something might scare you out of your wits; so good night, Mr. Clipper." With a sort of mock bow she left him standing near the gate as she tripped off to her house with the canary, but not deigning to notice the string of pickerel lying stark in the evening dew.

He went down the bluff to his lonely shanty, where he sat for a long time before retiring, thinking of the reception his hard-hearted love had given him; of her unyielding obstinancy toward him, her cruel suspicions in regard to a covert wish of bettering his condition financially by an alliance with her; and, worse than all, her contemptous insinuations as to his being a coward.

She had treated both him and his proposal with down-right meanness, that was certain, and he about half made up his mind that night to forget all about her, even if he had to leave the place to do it.

Hannah went back and got the fish after her much misused lover had disappeared in the gloaming. She did it for two reasons, one was that she was fond of them, and the other that a part of her domestic education had been to never allow anything to go to waste. So, after she had cleaned and salted them she put them away for her breakfast the next morning, after which she went into her little front parlor and sat down on her cretonne-covered rocker with her knitting in her hand.

She rocked, and knit, and thought.

Somehow she had an unusually dissatisfied feeling whenever her mind reverted toward the scene in the flower-garden, and she could not remember a time when mature reflection had showed her conduct up in so bad a manner. She was about half way remorseful for her treatment of William, for whom she really had some liking; more than she had for any one since she lost her fair young lover away back in the war days at the battle of Gettysburg.

That event had gone a long way toward making Hannah the odd creature she was, as she never quite got over the sorrowful heart-break which came to her then; and instead of making her more sweet-tempered by the patience wrought of sorrow, as some would have been, it had the reverse effect of making her rather cross and cynical in her disposition.

The more her eyes wandered toward the sleeping bird in its cage, which she had hung far up on a nail by the window from the reach of the cat, the more she thought of his affectionate kindness in buying it for her; and, then, she remembered his imperturbable demeanor under the shower of her insults and sneers, and wondered whether in all the world there existed another so forbearing a man. In her own mind she was convinced that he did care for her and not for her small property as she had told him, and she almost pursuaded herself that if he were not quite so shiftless and would give up his vagabondish ways for something more respectable, she might be induced to think seriously of his offer.

Her premises were running down for want of some one to keep them in order, some one possessed of more strength than she had in her arms; and the milking of her cow for year in and year out was becoming burdensome to her, and, what was still worse—for her lonely situation—tramps were getting quite numerous around, so that she might be murdered any night and her nearest neighbor not be able to hear from her or give her aid, being a good stone's throw away.

There was no need, however, of her being alone, as many had been the orphan or deserted waif commended to her by well-meaning people, as an object upon which to bestow her care, but she

considered herself as being too wise a woman to
listen to any of their plans.

She had known enough of such cases, she said,
to be fully satisfied that the person who took a
child of that sort, was, but in extremely rare
instances, never thanked for their pains. There
were always mischievous people to be found,
ready and willing to put a variance between the
benefited and the benefactor; mostly to the dis-
advantage of the latter, so she did not care to run
the risk of getting herself into trouble of that
kind.

Thus on account of a class to be found the world
over, a class who are perhaps more thoughtless
or incapable of seeing things in proper light than
wicked, some poor child was prevented from a
comfortable home.

The spinster had never before so felt the loneli-
ness of her single life like she did this night, as
she heard the low tick of the clock and listened to
the gentle sweep of the wind across the windows.

George Washington, on the wall opposite,
seemed to have a sterner look than usual about
his always firm mouth, and the face of Abraham
Lincoln, looking down at her from above, appeared
to wear a sadder look than she had noticed before.

Even the bit of fine landscape painting, with its
rising sun and soft tints, for which she had paid
quite a bit of money to Eldie—her neighbor artist
—had lost its brightness, and the room with all its
adornments had a sort of undefined failure about
it to make her as fully satisfied with herself and

her home as previously, and before she retired for the night she almost persuaded herself that if her lover came again to offer her his hand in marriage she should accept it at once.

CHAPTER III.

The next morning Clipper, arrayed in his best called at the home of Mrs. Desmond to get the carriage and directions to go after Miss Dudley.

She came in full glory.

She almost took the breath away from her escort as he handed her into the seat behind him, for he, poor man, in his humble life, did not very often come in contact with fine ladies, and here was one, indeed.

From furtive glances cast backward, Clipper caught a flash of shimmering lace and bright ribbons, a glitter of bijou ornamentation and the scintillation of diamonds, with a coquettish face, flower-like in its delicate coloring, as seen through the fine mist of a dark veil.

"Rouge and pearl powder," thought the driver in a ruminating sort of way, as a sweet violet scent assailed his senses, from the seat behind him; "they all use it, these fashionable belles," and then his mental vision involuntarily went out toward cruel, heartless Hannah, who was too good a woman to make use of any such deceptive means; and if her face was not the most alluring in the world, it was a real and a sincere one.

But no more of that. His heart was yet sorely suffering from her rude words, and he took then

and there a firm resolve to take no more retrospec-
tive views, so commenced to study the blocks of
Kasota and sandstone in the facades as he passed
along, and to consider how graciously nature had
arrayed all her works for the benefit of mankind
in both a useful and ornamental way.

"You have a beautiful city," said the lady, bend-
ing slightly forward to make her remark the more
easily understood, and then drawing herself suddenly back as if half ashamed at her boldness in
thus venturing upon a first remark to her *biz-
arre* companion.

"Yes," he replied, with a slight bow of his head,
as he touched his hat with old-fashioned courtesy.
"It is thought by some to be as handsome as any
place in the country. But, as the saying goes,
handsome is that handsome does, and I can say
that she can fill that axiom, too, for she is just as
flourishing as she is fine appearing," and Clipper
went off into the pardonable and usual extrava-
gances pertaining to citizens of all places whose
growth has been unusually rapid and prosperous.

Hetty was surprised at the elegance of his language, so inconsistent with his superficial appearance, and really it was better than that of most of
the fine men of wealth and position that she had
met in her social intercourse with the world.

Why should it be otherwise?

Clipper had spent his time in the pursuit of such
reading and studies which cannot do otherwise
than leave their elevating mark upon mind and
speech, and while other men had given their

attention toward business and the most approved
business methods, to the end that they might get
riches and worldly honor, he had been content
to know no more in that way than would suffice
his daily wants, while his exceptionally deep love
of nature and her works had kept his mind as
pure as that of a woman.

He was Nature's gentleman, without alloy.

The fine points of the city described, its mani-
fold praises exhausted, the two occupants of the
carriage again fell into silence ; but all the while
Hetty, from behind, was watching the queer cut
and style of Clipper's coat, and wondering what
sort of a man he must be, that could talk so well,
and yet dress so shabbily. He was thinking that
she was a charming woman to converse with, and
apparently not at all proud and snobbish, as he at
first thought she must be.

Of a sudden the vehicle stopped.

Clipper got out amidst a pile of broken imported
rock, which some workmen were busy in assort-
ing, and, picking a piece from the debris, returned
to the carriage with it in his palm.

The bit of stone was ordinary enough, to a common observer, and only a virtuosa, bent on looking always for something to gratify his passion,
would have detected anything in it, among the
rest of its kind.

But to him it was a most rare treasure, being of
dendritic formation, and containing in its trans-
parent depth, as if reflected in a mirror, a well defined landscape view of a small lake or pond, sur-

rounded by rushes and sedge grass, with a background of willows and other trees.

Dioptrics had caught the shadow, and finding a proper mineral and chemical condition, had prepared, according to Nature's mystery, upon the face of the rock, an indelible picture, long before Dagnerre found out the science of actinism.

He turned about and handed it to his companion, explaining to her his idea of the cause of the strange picture.

But Hetty took but little interest in it.

She was not of the sort who could rank among the number of those who, according to the poet, " read sermons in stones."

A piece of music, upon which were recorded the notes for a new galop or quadrille, would have been far more to her fancy, for, if not a virtuosa, like Clipper, she was certainly one of another kind, at least to a limited extent, as, for instance, a love of the pursuit of Orpheus, when it contributed toward the glories of the ball-room, and a love of color, when found among velvet and other goods used for fashionable adornment.

To please the queer man, however, she affected an admiration for his curiosity, and, as she was an adept in the art of dissimulation, she quite undeceived him as to her true apathy in the matter; and he received it from her with the assurance that she quite sympathized with him in his philosophical fancies, a thing he was sure Hannah —. There he checked his thoughts as completely as

if they had been as well under control as the
sleek pair of chestnuts in front of him were to bit
and bridle.   It was hard, though, to keep Hannah
altogether out of his mind.

The purlieu of the city gained, they were not
long in running over the gravelly road of the lake
shore, and up the bit of elevation leading to the
Desmond cottage.

There they were met by its mistress and her
two daughters, who were on the look-out for their
coming.

That lady was slightly surprised, in a most
agreeable manner, however, at finding her niece
even more handsome and distinguished looking
than she had viewed her mentally.

It was quite a number of years since she had
parted from her in the East, in a manufacturing
town in Pennsylvania, at a time when the girl—
now a woman of twenty-five — was but fifteen
years old.   An uninterrupted correspondence during the interval had kept her well informed as to
all affairs connected with her brother's family,
and, of course, Hetty's social triumphs as a belle,
along with the rest.

She was certainly most royally beautiful, she
thought, as she eyed her gracefully rounded form;
and proud poise of shoulders, neck and head.
Langtry, whom she had once seen, could not be a
peer with her, she was sure ; and she doubted
whether in all the adjacent city and country,
filled, as it was, with fair women, her equal in
appearance could be found.

She was flattered by the thought of being aunt to so fair a creature, and cared not a whit that her own twins were quite thrown into the shade by a star so magnificent, partly because petty jealousy was not among the list of her weaknesses, and partly because she, as yet, looked upon them as little more than children.

And Charles Lennox? How must he be affected by her beauty, when once he should meet her? She wondered about it, and thought that his surprise must be as great as her own, when he should see how much superior to her picture she really was. Then a cloud came over her musings, as the suggestion intruded itself that the likelihood was that more than surprise would take possession of him; and thus Eldie would be left free for John's wooing.

Upon the third evening after the coming of her niece, she gave a small neighborhood entertainment for the unmarried folks, as a means of an introduction of the new-comer among them.

She could not well slight Eldie Janneaux, so she sent to her a note of invitation; but the young artist plead another engagement, and so excused her presence upon the occasion.

Charles Lennox was there, to be sure, along with a score or more of ladies and gentlemen, among them William Clipper and Major Stewart, also a bachelor.

Between the first of these two and his hostess there was no rythm.

Their ideas could never harmonize, being as widely diversant as the poles of the earth.

To her his unconventional mode of life was disgusting in the extreme; his religious and political creeds, *outre* and isolated; while to him she was a most lively representative of what is said to be the worst of all fools, an old fool, with her narrow views, limited on all sides by weakness and selfishness, and her futile grasping after the unattainable in wealth and social position.

She invited him, however, to Her small party, out of compliment for his kindnes in bringing Hetty from the train, at a time when John was suddenly called upon to attend a law suit in regard to a complication in which some of his land was involved. Clipper accepted the invitation for the reason that he was glad to go to any place in which some excitement was promised, in order that by this means he might better be enabled to drive the thoughts of Hannah from his mind.

That personage was not invited, because Mrs. Desmond hardly thought that the spinster would take the kindness acceptably, and indeed her absence was quite more agreeable to the lady than her presence would be.

They were no warm friends, these two women, of whom it may be said that both were possessed of an equal amount of pride and obstinacy, but in directions quite different.

Mrs. Desmond was proud, and she considered it her divine right to be so, descended as she was from people who, to use her own expression, "had

always been able to hold their heads up along
with the best," and who had been of the landed
aristocracy of the Keystone State, where to own a
good farm is considered of much more importance
than in states where land is more readily obtained.

Hannah, too, was proud, but the more aristocratic women opposed it strenuously. She
thought it quite out of place in her, as being the
daughter of a day laborer—Hannah had told her
so much herself—and considered her as wanting
in the graces which a better position might have
given to her.

The spinster was full of the sharpness of speech
usual to persons of her temperament, made forcible at times by a vigorous mode of expression,
and, what was still more offensive, her reason,
though uncultured, was yet sufficiently clear to
censure the semi-intriguing ways and follies of
her opponent; and her criticisms were not confined
to her own bosom, altogether, but with her keen
tongue she voiced them whenever she chose.

Her spirit was indomitable, for Hannah was an
American, and, along with the most of her people
she was possessed with the feeling given to them
as a legacy from that spirit which breathed into
the constitution with the words, "all are born free
and equal," also the self-respect not to be found
elsewhere among the masses, the wonder, sometimes the disgust, of foreigners.

So Hannah was not among the guests at the
lakeside cottage, but those who were there passed
a very enjoyable time.

Henrietta Dudley, a most magnificent woman, not only in the eyes of her aunt, but, indeed, in the eyes of all who beheld her, had carried off the palm of beauty in gatherings the most choice and fashionable, so was, to this semi-rural party, simply wonderful in the admiration that she excited.

Her eyes were blue, but looked almost purple by the effect produced by long, dark eye lashes, with an animated sparkle in their clear depths, as if life were to their owner all free from care or grief. They shed a glorious light over the shell-like complexion, upon which was no token of the cosmetics that Clipper had been so ready to impute to it. Her features were slightly irregular, and if her brow was low enough to escape any great intellectuality, yet it was surely a most smooth and fair one, surmounted, as it was, by heavy rolls of hair, of a sombre, bronze-brown hue.

In height she was somewhat above the medium size of women, with a form neither too slender nor too full, and walking or sitting the poise of her neck and head was both graceful and majestic.

She was dressed in the most exquisite and faultless taste, in a robe of rose-pink silk, with drapings of black lace, a single diamond pin at her throat and another glittering among the meshes of her hair—nothing very grand or expensive, but well suited to her simple surroundings.

She understood the art of personal adornment to perfection, and was possessed of a fine ward-

robe with which to display her skill, as John, who
had brought it from the depot the day before,
could well testify, if he were allowed to judge
from the quantity and weight of her trunks.

A party of six, among them young Orme and
the twin sisters, were amusing themselves with a
game of dominos, nothing that savored more of
gambling being allowed by the pseudo Christian
entertainer.

Euchre was hinted at, but the daughters gave
the guests to know their mother's views, and so
they said no more on the subject.

John sat quiet, as usual, and rather moody, too,
on account of the absence of Eldie; while Lennox
and Miss Dudley, by request, occupied the piano,
either alternately or together, the rest of the young
people being but indifferent performers upon it.

Major Stewart and Clipper, not caring for the
goddess calliope, neither for any of the games
and tete-a-tetes of the more youthful part of the
assembly; strolled out into a side porch, shaded
by vines, where they might enjoy the cool evening breeze, a cigar and a quiet chat to themselves.

Not that there was any great likeness between
the two men, unless it might be a fellow feeling,
engendered by their bachelorhood, for in all other
respects, they were quite different, although both
were possessed of considerable intellectual
acumen, each in his own way.

Their conversation soon drifted into an argu-
mentative channel, as the major was by nature a
controversalist.

Having never made religion his study, he was
out as a polemic there, but give to him politics,
history, or the bearing of society at large, and few
could equal, none surpass him upon these subjects, while his words flowed as readily as does
the stream on its course.

He was rather exclusive in his ideas, and was
possessed of a degree of hauteur, which matched
not badly with his fine physique and military
bearing: nor yet with his claim of royal blood
which had come down to him from the old gener-
ation of Scottish kings whose name he bore.

"We are," he said, after the conversation had
been fairly opened, "passing, as a people, through
a stage of transition. The time will come—in
truth it already begins to cast fitful gleams across
our horizon—when we, no longer a confused mass
of human beings, will be as clearly and firmly
defined, in our several stations, as are the classes
of the Old World."

"And would you," asked Clipper, "think a condition of that sort an improvement upon our
present social style ? "

The major reflected awhile before answering
this question, so openly and pointedly put.

"Yes," he at length said ; "I cannot help but
consider a condition of the kind mentioned to be
a better one than is this of the present; a state of
unlimited freedom, where every one, of either sex,
or any station, is at full liberty to enter the whirl-
pool of ambitious design. Existence is thus rendered one of perpetual strife and turmoil, each

elbowing the other in order to get one step ahead
on the ladder of advancement, and this uncon-
fined sway may be set down as the cause of the
vast empiricism to be found among all the arts,
trades and professions of the present day."

"In the time of revolutionary fame, when so
many good and grand lives were lost for this one
principle of individual liberty, you would, with
such sentiments, have been euphoniously de-
nounced as a royalist, to save you from a name
more harsh; and I, at this time, can look upon you
in no other light than that of a monarchist impa-
tient for a kingly power to be set over us."

"You do not understand aright the purport of
my words, nor the feeling which dictated them.
None would be more averse to a crowned head
and a sceptered hand as a representation of our
government. Yet I still maintain that liberty is,
in many respects, taken as a license rather, and
that more of a restraint should be exercised in our
social system, in order to regulate matters for the
suppression of error."

"That idea is certainly well enough, but this
reform must be accomplished without the forming of class distinctions. Civil liberty is the watchword of republican principles, and not for a select
set only, but for the whole body of the people;
and the more the wealth of the country changes
from a collective to an inherited state, just in pro-
portion must this watchword be preserved and
intensified, in order to keep our system intact as
it came from the hands of its founders. Let us

allow the spirit of caste to remain where it is, in
the empires across the sea, until these people become sufficiently enlightened to cast off its yoke."

Clipper had, during his little speech, assumed
an animation altogether at variance with his
usual placid demeanor, so that his listener was
both amused and astonished at his argumenta-
tive force, so unusual in one of his manner of
life, but here his interest ended.

It had power neither to pique him to a further display of his own ability nor to convince
him of truth.

He looked upon the fisherman as one of earth's
unfortunate ones, who would crave the gold trans-
forming touch of Midas as much as any, could he
but have it; and considered his contempt of
riches and of the aristocracy produced by it, as
but the outcome of his weakness and inability to
obtain these things himself.

The evening was growing chilly, a damp mist
was arising from the lake, so they left the outside
for the warmth of the house.

In the small parlor the young people were still
over their game, which had, however, been
changed from dominos to chess.

John had retired, as had likewise some of
the guests, but Henrietta and Charles still lin-
gered at the piano and music sheets, engaged in
spirited argument over the merits of the different styles of composition.

Henrietta liked the mode of the modern school,
but Charles had a decided and well defined pre-

erence for that of a decade or two ago, even allowing his backward prejudice to take so free a
scope until they came to the impassioned and
poetic themes of the great Scottish bard.

He was speaking now of his songs, the particular one being the well worn one, "Afton Water,"
and he was loud in his praise of the exquisite
description of nature and lofty sentiments therein
embodied.

"Where," he said, "among all the sentimental
and frivolous songs of our time, can anything like
its equal be found?

"Either our song-writers of the present day
are altogether devoid of the true instinct of
their art, or else the public taste is so vitiated
and weakened by the hum-drum, ultra-practical
walk of modern life, that they can appreciate
nothing better. There is," he went on to say,
"a great deal of talk about the liberality of this
epoch toward people of literary ability, or literary tendencies, if you will, but I fancy did a
Burns, a Goldsmith, or any other penniless and
unprestiged bard arise among us his struggles
would be as great, or even greater, than did those
men of genius encounter during their lives.
Rodomontade has more of a footing among us
than would, without thoughtful consideration, be
supposed. Yes, we are an unmitigated nation of
braggarts!"

"Why, how you speak!" said Henrietta, laying
her jewelled finger upon his arm with as much
familiarity as if she had known him for years, in-

stead of a few hours, as she looked him full in the face with her fine eyes—were there ever such eyes? thought her companion.

"I'm sure I can not see what fault you have to find with our present melodies. I think them delightful; but, to be sure, I know but little of the poets you speak of, or of their works. If I did it might make a difference. I like one or two old songs, "Robin Adair," for instance. That *is* a fine song—so much of womanly feeling and constancy breathing through its lines; there is inspiration, true and natural, for you. Shall I sing it?"

Charles would have allowed her to sing anything and every thing, no matter how long the time consumed, so delightfully sweet did he find it to be near her.

Her aunt, he mused, was right, as he watched her fingers running lightly over the keys, and the delicate curve of her neck and chin, as with a clear, full voice, she trilled her favorite song.

"She is a charming woman, certainly, the most charming I ever met, be her nose retrousse or Grecian; but it is neither, it is rather an intermediate form, and, indeed, no other sort would harmonize with the fine lineaments of her face."

The plain, unvarnished truth—as some old chronicler would say—was that the man was fairly in love for the first time in his life, and that with this fascinating creature of so short acquaintance, and of whose antecedants he knew so little.

Farewell, Madame Desmond, to all your cherished schemes for presenting a thing of this sort!

Farewell to your plans for keeping John from the pale-faced artist girl! She is now his to woo, to win and to marry, for anything that Charles Lennox will do to prevent.

He had never loved her.

Admiration is not love, and respect is not love ; he found it to-night for the first time in his life, and found, too, that, fine and elevated as they are, they yet contain none of the ecstatic joys which the blind little winged god, Cupid, can confer upon whom he sees fit to rest in his blind flight.

He had imagined that he thought a great deal of Eldie, but that it was only in a brotherly way, and not after the fashion of a man's love for the woman he would make his wife, was fully demonstrated to his heart to-night. Every Adam should have an Eve, and this was his Eve, or else none existed for him—most dismal thought ; but he hoped for a better fortune.

He deprecated the bitter seeds so apt to be strewn by a malicious and envious fate among the ambrosial food upon which lovers dine.

The elfin sprit was busy, also, in another corner of the room.

It was where Major Stewart had seated himself at the little chess table, and was talking in his grandiose, cavalier-like way to the small group of players about the success of their game, as to how many had lost, or how many had won, and was the number of each about even ?

Anna Desmond, he found, was the trump in the affair, and it pleased him greatly.

He had always liked the twins, whom he met on his frequent visits to see his old friend and schoolmate, Alfred Desmond, but of late he seemed to be drifting m re toward Anna in his affections; thus leaving her sister the least bit to the larboard side, in sailors' parlance.

But this night may be set down as the deciding turn of his passion for the fair-haired, timid damsel, who might have been his daughter, and a few years to spare.

He had been in love many a time before, during the years of his gallant and debonair life—that is, such a love as is usual to a man of his cold, proud temperament: a love which time and a little separation soon cools, so that he had, notwithstanding these many times, never been long enough in the toils to allow himself to enter the list matrimonial.

The object of his wavering fancy had, it seemed, this time left a more abiding impression than usual, and he meant to ask her hand in marriage in less than a year. Time did not seriously intervene in the way of prevention.

In a short time the remaining guests took their departure, each wending his way homeward, among them Major Stewart, to his city boarding-house, Charles Lennox to the comfortable farm-house of his maternal relative, and Clipper to his wood-embowered hut.

Three men in the condition amo, but each with a piece of femininity widely differing in character.

CHAPTER IV.

A tea party was inaugurated at the home of Hannah.

Not that the worthy woman often indulged in anything of that sort, but the days were tedious in that out-lying district from which few excursions could be made into the city; and then, along with the consideration of doing something to enliven her neighbors somewhat, there was the more practical one of by this means, having all those carpet rags sewed, which she would so badly need in the spring!

It was a sensible way of hitting two birds with one stone, and has always been prevalent in rural parts.

It is about as good a way for the dissemination of news as any lover of gossip could wish.

At this gathering were Mrs. Fairchild, Mrs. Weston, Mrs. Finch and Mrs. Babbit—principal ladies of the community—with a dozen, perhaps, of the wall-flower kind, who, in their butter-cup modesty, were quite over-shadowed by their more brilliant, sun-flower sisters.

"Did you hear," asked Mrs. Weston, after the conversation had been fairly launched, "that Charles Lennox is quite taken with that niece of Mrs. Desmond?"

"Yes, I have heard it," answered one of the principals.

"Well, I don't wonder that he is," meekly put in one of the wall-flowers, "for she is so handsome."

"'Handsome is that handsome does' is an old and true saying," said the first speaker, a little sharply, with a keen look toward her of the wall, as if to warn her not to venture too far out of her place.

"I guess that aphorism will suit Miss Dudley, also," said Mrs. Fairchild, "as she seems to be a lady in the true sense of that much abused word."

"Distinguished looking, too," added Mrs. Weston; "seems to have a good deal of mental force, held in reserve, of course, as any woman of refinement would keep it."

"And why in reserve?" ventured a wall-flower.

"In reserve, because no true lady cares to bring out ability of that sort, and, if possessed of it, merely keeps it as a sort of fund, upon which she might fall back, in case fortune should turn an iron front to her, or her money take wings and fly off, as it sometimes does from the best regulated of human beings."

"That is a poor figure to apply to money—I mean of its 'flying off.' Now, money that would so act, must needs all be in paper; gold and silver would never take wings."

"Well then sink into the earth, I will say, if that suits your idea better; or it might pass into the hands of a thief or a mortgagor, not that I consider the two synonymous—far from it."

"Not a great deal of difference, sometimes," said Mrs. Finch.

"I know of a family in the neighborhood who have hypothecated their furniture through necessity occasioned by sickness and other misfortunes, and the interest is so great that it is all they can do to keep it paid; with no prospect of being able to raise the principal, thus living with a two-edged sword, as it were, continually suspended, by the merest thread, above them; and their mortgagor, instead of mercifully allowing them a way out of the difficulty, just keeps preying upon their earnings even though they starve for it. A human shark, he is, and nothing less!"

"Well, Mrs. Finch," said Mrs. Fairchild, "if you had money to loan, wouldn't you feel like getting all you could for it? I am sure that I should, and consider nothing unjust in so doing."

"A veritable Shylock you would be."

"A veritable just person I should be, that is all. There is entirely too much idle sympathy expended upon persons of that sort, for, as a general thing, they are altogether unworthy of it. Why do they get in arrears, that is what I want to know. It is strange that such cannot manage to get along without borrowing money of others."

"I think the conversation is becoming rather desultory," said Mrs. Babbit; "it has a vagrant tendency of which I do not approve altogether."

"It has become a little spidery, but we can easily draw the web back to its former position.

Let's see; I believe we were talking of the fair stranger, Miss Dudley."

"You were speaking," said a wall-flower, who seemed to be possessed of a little more spirit than her sisters, "of certain resources of the young lady, which might be brought to the surface, in case she were reduced to poverty, after she ceased to be a lady. Now, I always have been under the impression that the parts which go to form a woman worthy of the title, would remain with her equally in indigence or affluence."

"I see," said Mrs. Fairchild, "that you are in keeping with the Websterian definition—'Lady : a woman of education and refined manner'—but that has become obsolete. When Webster wrote that, he had no idea of the future. He knew not of a time when, through the beneficence of our free school plan, every tatterdemalian's child would become educated, and as to manners, why, they are easily enough acquired, so that if the ideas which were prevalent upon the subject several years ago were still in force, we should have every laborer's wife and every serving girl a lady. A queer state of affairs, truly."

"Nevertheless," said her opponent, who had herself been a teacher in the public schools, " I believe that our good Sexeographer was right, and that those qualifications mark the lady in any station of life. Such views as you advance, Mrs. Fairchild, would bring us back to the dark ages, indeed they would. I don't know what to make of them, unless they symbolize the 'abomination

of desolation,' spoken of in the New Testament,
which is to proclaim the near end of time."

"I guess you have been among the Advent
people."

"No, I have not."

"But, to return once more, does any one suppose that it will be a match between Charlie and
the fair Pennsylvahian?"

"I for one can't say, I am sure. She may be
good enough for him, but perhaps his mother will
not think so. It is said that her father is a heavy
owner in mine stock out east, and consequently
she is rich enough; but old Mrs. Lennox is a
stickler for blood, you see."

"As to her blood I don't know; but I am sure her
dresses and jewelry fully bear out the assertion
about her father's riches," said a wall-flower, with
a sort of frightened gasp at the end of her
sentence, as if to say, "O! there, I have spoken too
much for me."

"Yes, certainly all appears well enough that
way, but the Lennox family, I imagine, will look
for good descent. They, themselves, claim rela-
tionship with Captain Lennox, of Vermont. He
was a great military light in the war of the Revolution, not Rebellion, as an English woman once
had the impudence to call it in my presence; but
I told her that the terms had a different meaning
attached to them. A revolution is a successful
revolt, and its followers are styled heroes; but, if
unsuccessful, it is a rebellion, and its followers are
called rebels."

"Well, as I was saying, this Captain Lennox traced his lineage away back among the Scottish nobility, to the time when one of his female ancestors received as a gift for her undaunted loyalty as much land as she could walk around while her fugitive monarch, Robert Bruce, and a companion of his, ate their breakfast in her sheeling. The good dame, being tall and masculine, took long and rapid strides, and so compassed more of the bargain than the king would have thought possible in the time; but he was in for it, as the saying is, and from that time on her family were the Lennox, of Lennox Brae, County of Galloway. So much is to be found in the legends of those parts."

"Now these Pennsylvania people have, for the most part, no claims to good descent, in fact, think very little about it. I know, as I once lived among them."

"They have a good deal of superstition, though, have'nt they?" asked Mrs. Weston.

"Superstition? I should say they have!"

"Not, of course, among the better informed class, but among the common people, especially those of German origin. Why, I know a family that lived for ten years in a house which, according to their saying, was haunted in the worst kind of a way!"

"Wonderful were the tales they had to relate of a woman in white, to be met on dark nights in chamber and stairway or along corridor; of the stain of blood in one of the rooms which no scouring could erase, and the many and mysterious noises to be heard at almost all seasons!"

"There was an old mill a few rods from the house, which, in its day, had done substantial duty by supplying the neighborhood with flour, but had been in a decaying condition for many years."

"The machinery of this mill, or what still remained of it, would, they averred, start up at the most uncanny hour of the night with a clang and rattle, as if the demons at work with it meant to be heard, if not seen!"

"I should have felt like getting out of that place as soon as I could," said Mrs. Babbit. "Were they honest people?"

"Yes, they were thoroughly honest and religious as well. They really must have been sincere in their belief of the marvels."

"To prove that they were not alone in the matter, when, upon their removal to a new house of their own, another family took possession of the vacated premises, strangers, mind you, from a distant section, they would not stay in it at all, but left after an occupancy of two days. From that on the old place fell to pieces through neglect and decay."

"Strange it is," said Mrs. Finch, "that any one should be found in this age of intellectual advance, holding ideas of that sort; for I claim that we do march onward in the right direction, old fogies and croakers to the contrary nevertheless."

"Most certainly, we do live in a progressive age, as I said to William Clipper the other day when he came to my house with some fish. By the way, what provokingly odd ideas that man does have on a good many subjects. Do you know that he had the audacity to tell me the other day that it was just as much of a sin to enter into the absolute pursuit of riches as it was to break any one of the ten commandments, and should be considered as disgraceful!"

"He furthermore said that the latter came from God through the medium, Moses, a man only; but that the saying in regard to a love of riches came directly from God's son!"

"That was queer talk," said Mrs. Weston.

"He spoke about the ministers, too, and pointed to the way in which they all, or most of them— for he made some allowance as an exception— made out to get as far away from the subject of Dives and Lazerus, or of the camel and the needle's eye as possible."

"I presume," said Mrs. Babbit, "that any clergyman who would take up as a theme, propositions of that sort, would at once make himself exceedingly unpopular. The skillful minister will seek to explain the doings of Joshua, David or the Prophets, rather than to touch upon topics suitable to the present day, for, by so doing, he keeps upon safe ground."

"That was precisely Clipper's argument."

"Clipper is a fool," said Mrs. Finch; "but have you heard," she continued, in a suppressed tone, "that he has designs this way?"

"Yes, I have heard as much," answered the leader, "but I presume he might as well spare himself his pains. Hannah is far too sensible a woman to unite in marriage with a man as shiftless and nonsensical as he is. But do look out of the window, and tell me whether that is Mrs. Flemming, or is it some one else?"

"It is Mrs. Flemming," answered some one.

"Where can she be going? Perhaps to my house, and she will find no one at home. She comes there sometimes to get newspapers to cover the shelves of her pantry. She said, the last time she was up, that she did wish that Flemming would take a paper, so she might then have material for cutting patterns and such like."

"Dear me," said Mrs. Babbitt, "and does she never find time to read anything of the sort?"

"How could she, my dear, with all of her family to work for, and the worthlessness of her husband to contend against as well?"

"What is the number of them? A great many, I am sure, by the troop I have seen playing about the door."

"There are just eleven of them," answered Mrs. Weston, "all quite young, Agnes, the eldest, being but seventeen."

As the gathering was exclusively American, among whom, as a race, a family of like quantity is a very rare exception, it caused a laugh to arise among the central group, which sent its vibrations back to the walls, in about the same way that circular waves swell and fall when water is disturbed by some heavy body.

"She preserves her health," said the leader.

The laugh rose louder than before.

They all seemed to understand the signification of the sentence.

"I heard," said one of the wall-flowers, "that Flemming is working on a new invention; some sort of a wheel, a turbine, I think they call it, and some of his neighbors do think that he will make a success of it. I for one wish he would, for the sake of his family, if nothing else."

"A plague upon his inventions, every one of them, I say, for the time which he has thrown away upon them. Why does he not look about for something more practical? It is the fruit of those dreamy ideas of his that is continually throwing his family into want. Why, I have been told that the girl, Agnes, keeps the breath in them all by the meagre wages of a mill-worker, which is limited, miserable as it is, by the amount paid out for car fare to and from the city."

Then the leader arose, as she finished her sentence, shook the fragments of cloth from her apron into the rag-basket, while she glanced around the room to see in what manner the work was getting along. As the four principals had done nearly all of the talking, the greater part of the sewing had been accomplished by the more retiring members of the assembly.

"Ladies, I am afraid you are not winding your rags just right," she said, "you should always put the brightest colors on the outside, only for the looks, of course, but looks, you know, go a great way in all things."

"I can't see what difference it can make in a ball of carpet rags," a little spitefully put in a wallflower.

"Well, it does make a difference."

"Yes, I know it does," said Mrs. Finch, "because a weaver is apt to judge character from just so small a standpoint. The person who sends carelessly prepared rags to him, will receive in return a poorly woven carpet. 'Straws,' as the saying is, 'show which way the wind blows,' and human nature is so constructed that the slack and untidy will continually be imposed upon."

"Now, I call that sort of talk deeply logical," said Mrs. Babbit, in a pleasantly ironical way, "it might even take down Plato himself, were he here, and if any of us were spiritualists, we might suppose his ethereal presence, and even go so far as to say that he put that very wise thought, as to cause and effect, into your head."

There was another laugh at this sally of wit.

"However, we are not spiritualists, thanks to a happy horoscope for each of us," said Mrs. Weston, "and what a good thing it is that the abominable doctrine has never taken root in this neighborhood. Why, I have heard of more scandals, divorces, and what not, engendered among families by this belief, than from any other cause. Yet I cannot explain the reason why a faith in the communion of the dead with the living should have anything to do with looseness of morals, free-love, and, in the words of an old lady acquaintance of mine, 'a general queerity of mind.' "

"That is not true spiritualism," said a bright little woman. "True spiritualism is one of the holiest and ennobling of beliefs, and is taught by all churches, if not directly, still by implication. What more sublime than the ancient creed of the Communion of Saints, as taught by the early fathers?"

"Yes, but modern spiritualism is supposed by its followers to be based upon some occult, philosophical law, which time will, in all probability, so develop that all may understand its workings. Of course, I am no advocate for its mysteries; I merely retail what has been told to me by those who are."

"Philosophy or no philosophy," said Mrs. Finch, "it in no manner agrees with divine writing. True, the Saviour did see Moses and Elias, as did also the several disciples, but the vision was directly brought to them by sacred influence. What wicked presumption it must be for any mere mortal to assume the powers of Christ! and that is just what all are doing who profess to be able to call into their presence disembodied spirits. Believe me, it is all the work of Satan!"

"But," said Mrs. Fairchild, "divine writing is rather indefinite in many ways, and—in the field of scientific truth—the church has committed her errors, as we only have to cite history to prove. Her suffering outcast, Galonelileo, is one notable instance of her entire fallibility in the matter. Now I, for one, do not care to condemn a doctrine or theory of which I know nothing, because, from this very fact of my ignorance in the matter, I am not capable to judge. I am, in this respect, like a physician I once knew out among the fore-mentioned devotees of vulgar metaphysics, or, in plainer terms, spook seers, if I may so call them. In the course of practice he often came to a patient who, along with his own skill, had also called in that of a neighbor, who could stop the course of disease by incantations or pow-wowing, as it is called in those parts. The good doctor paid no heed, whatever, so long as they did nothing contrary to his directions, upon the thought that if they did no good, they could do no harm."

"Quite kind of him;" said Mrs. Finch. "I know of some of the class who would at once have donned their cloak of Esculapian dignity; and have ordered the conjurors from his patients, or else resigned all care of them."

At this moment the spare face of Hannah was seen at the door to invite them out into the dining room to tea.

The good woman had her own ideas of how guests ought to be treated. No lap lunches for her!

They were entirely too meagre in the way of refreshment and gave, she would say, an appearance of either stinginess or laziness on the part of the hostess, either of which abstract qualities she utterly abhorred.

Hannah was not stingy in all cases where her judgment told her that liberality was proper, nor was she lazy because an indulgence in that way would have compromised the title she had earned of the best house-keeper in the neighborhood; and no statesman of eminence was more proud of his position than she of hers, in her proper sphere.

Therefore, the supper was a marvel of culinary skill, of abundance and variety. It was a dinner and supper combined, with roast fowl, cold ham and oysters by way of meats, a half dozen sorts of vegetables, pies, cakes, fruit and cream. Both hyson and mocha as a beverage, so that really the guests must have thought that "tea" was rather too light a name for a collation so extensive.

"Oh dear," said Mrs. Weston on the way home, "who would have expected to find a meal served up after that style. Why, one would suppose that Hannah had in view the victualing of a gang of bootblacks or some other equally hungry crowd."

"It's the custom in the part of the east where she came from. There they live to eat instead of eating to live, as the saying goes. The three-fold nature of human existence is scarcely recognized. The intellectual is but scantily cultivated; the moral or spiritual perhaps a little more, but the physical is the one that preminently stands out in bold relief, as against the two other ones."

"Well, at any rate, I think we have all enjoyed ourselves at Hannah's," said Mrs. Finch. "She is a nice woman, and I hope that she will not throw herself away on that Clipper."

Here they had reached a separating point, whence each was to go in different directions to their several homes.

CHAPTER V.

It was June when Henrietta came among them, and it was now the latter part of September, the beautiful dreamy seventh month of the Latins, the month which in Northern climes takes the place that her later sister, October, does in lands lying further toward the tropics.

In the State of Minnesota it is a grand month, for now the heat of summer is modified by the least felt chills of the coming winter, outriders from the camp of the storm-king of the Arctic Zone, who has come to give warning of his approach, but as yet he is far off, and his weak messengers but add a charm where their commander means to desolate.

It was just the season for a man in love to think about picnics, excursions, or a boat ride by moonlight.

A day to be spent among the wildly rugged hills and upland lakes lying back of the farm boundaries was suggested by Lennox.

It was proposed that after a forenoon spent in rambling and fishing, they should all meet at a point where a woodland dinner, in true gypsy fashion, would be in readiness, under the care of two or three experts in such matters; among them Hannah who agreed to come, provided Clipper be excluded from the company, and, of course, she had her way, much to the annoyance of some of the company who considered her whim to be mere folly in keeping away a man who knew so much of the art of taking fish either by net or line.

Clipper was, however, in happy ignorance of his fair Dulcina's decision, as he had left the day before the affair came off to go on a hazelnut gathering, quite a distance away, and also to take a prospect as to the ginseng business during the coming year; for he really wished to do something to make Hannah think more of his money-making abilities than she did at present.

There were but eight couples invited, including the twins, Major Stewart, and a friend of his from the city; John and Eldie, Robert Orme and Agnes Flemming, Lennox and Henrietta, the remainder being composed of young farmers and their sweethearts.

The day was all that could be desired for the occasion, with a calmness sufficient for the great stretch of forest to seem one immense picture of Turner-like painting, with its brilliant hues of scarlet, orange, brown and russet, in all of their varied shades; only that Turner was in shadow when compared with the art here displayed, for, as the hand of some fatal disease will touch the cheek of lovliness with a more vivid and enhancing glow before his last destroying blow be given, so the great Autumn-painter spreads his tints with a lavish brush as a farewell feast of beauty and of color to the dying year.

And the skies! What mere human artist ever could produce the softly formed masses of white and of pearl, silently reposing on their bed of blue, or the fine lace-like filaments lying like a veil over the surface? Not one.

Art is, at best, but a poor imitation of nature; therefore, whoever would see it in its best sense must seek for it among the mystic depths of the forest, in the swelling roll of wave and billow, in the smooth surface of lake and river, or the changing hue of the sky and clouds.

Lennox enjoyed the scene more than he had ever before done anything of the sort, for, unlike Clipper or Orme, he usually cared but little for nature's work when unvarnished by the hand of man.

On this day all looked to him exceedingly fair.

Nothing, it seemed, could have power to dampen his ecstatic joy, engendered by these first days of passionate love, and he felt fully satisfied with himself and all of the world.

He revelled in a realm of dreamy happiness, broken only by a vague thought which would, at times, intrude itself, that, perhaps, after all his air castles, this gem among women, this peerless princess, might not be willing to accept him as a husband.

His mother had met her several times, and though well enough pleased at the prospect of a marriage between them, so far as Desmond's family went, yet, with a woman's instinct, she saw further into the character of her who might become her daughter-in-law than did her love-blind son.

She thought that she could detect symptoms of a cool, calculating mind, coupled with an un-principled heart under all of the wondrous beauty of the girl, and, at one time, ventured to suggest her thoughts to her son, but he would listen to no such talk, come it from whatever source it might.

He determined to-day to make to her a formal declaration of his love, with an offer of his hand and fortune, such as it was.

There were some misgivings on that score, of the last, but he would waive them for the present.

Marry first, to the woman he adored, and look as to a means of subsistence afterward.

That was the general way he had observed.

Few men ever thought of saving anything until after they were married. It seemed as though they were really unable to the task of laying away a dollar until after that portentious event.

Then, all of a sudden, as a maiden aunt of his used to say, "they make the wonderful discovery that what had been used to support one will now not only support two, with a prospective of a hand-ful of babies in a short time, but, also, leave a margin to save money upon!"

"Most glorious of paradoxes," she would add, "are these husbands!"

"Oh, how they want a woman to marry them for pure love of their own precious selves, and then the fortune that should, at least, have had a

beginning, must now be extracted from the bones
and blood of wife and little ones!"

These were her very words, he remembered, but
they should not influence him in his matrimonial
undertaking.

What were they, anyway, he reasoned, but the
senseless chatter of an unreasonable old maid,
who, perhaps, would only be too glad of the chance
to help some man to get on in the world!

During this mental soliloquy he was reclining
on the sloping bank of a small lake, at a point
where an everglade of brightest emerald run up
among the trees, and at whose top a knot of young
folks were industriously making garlands, of
golden-rod, asters, lupines and michaelmas daisies.

Hetty had fixed her rod and line for a bite of
pickerel or bass, and, with her hat laid aside, was
leisurely strolling along on the opposite side of
the water; stooping, at times, to pick up the tiny
spiral shells or shiny pebbles from the wet sand.

How enchanting she looked in her dress of
white mull and lace, with no ornament except a
bunch of crimson rose hips carelessly fixed among
the clusters of her hair; in gorgeous contrast to
the golden threads created among its dark bronze
by the sifted sun rays from the quivering
aspens above, and which gave to it the peculiar
tint so often seen in the Madonnas of the old
masters.

As she came around the bend of the bank
toward him, their eyes met, and she was near
enough for him to notice the slight flush, which

deepened the tint on cheek and lip, at the encounter.

She loves me, he thought. Oh, joy! This is an evidence, and now is my time to make sure of my happiness.

"Miss Dudley, or Hetty, which shall it be?"

"As you please," she answered, with a slight but graceful bow, "I am not at all formal where my friends are concerned."

Lennox arose and stood by her side.

She looked down upon the quiet water at her feet in a confused sort of way, as if, intuitively, she knew of his intention, and was at a loss how to act.

"Look," she said, in order to turn his thoughts into a different channel, "here is a cluster of senna, and yonder, in the shade of that boulder, are some gentian flowers. Blue and yellow; how do you like the contrast?"

"I know little of flowers," he replied, "and the mingling of their colors is the last thing to come into my thoughts at this time. I make human flowers my study, and you are the sweetest and fairest I have ever seen."

"You are a trifler, I fear," she said, looking gravely down again at the senna flowers in her hand.

"No trifler, I assure you," as he took her hand in his, and from this warm clasp she either had not the inclination to withdraw, or else the magnetism of this man was as the electric current acting upon a thing of life, and was altogether irresistible.

He was elated at her passiveness.

"And so," he resumed, "I am classed among your friends, Hetty! But I would be more than a friend! more than a brother! more than a father, even!"

"Do you hear me, Hetty?"

The head bent lower, the dye deepened over her face, but she made no answer.

"In plainer words, my darling, I would make you my wife to love and cherish, through all time. Indeed, such is the strength of my passion that I would willingly brave every danger for your sake, and should I be so unfortunate as to be called upon to lay your fair form in the cold bosom of earth, yet would my spirit follow you into the unknown realms and there claim you for my very own!"

Trembling with emotion, he clasped his arms about her still motionless and drooping figure.

"Shall it be, my Hetty, my love? Will you be my wife?"

"I will," she answered, raising her face to his; "that is, if nothing comes between us, if the fates will it."

"Thank you," he said fervently, with his whole heart in his words, as he stooped to kiss her upon brow and cheek, and for awhile he thought of nothing but the blissful fact that she had promised to be his.

After a while, as they walked forth and back along the strand, the provisional part of her promise came to him; "if nothing comes between us, if the fates allow it!"

Why should anything be allowed to come between them? He really wished it had been given a little more unconditional, but he mentally resolved to not run the risk of marring his present happiness by a mention of it.

A half hour fled on golden wings.

The fish had failed to take more than a nibble, but had done it so often, and so skillfully, that the bait was all consumed.

As they were about to cast out at a more convenient point, the sound of voices was wafted to their ears across the water, and looking toward the opposite shore they saw young Orme and Agnes Flemming sitting under the oaks, surrounded by heaps of flowers and mosses.

They had just came in from the rocky headlands back of them, where a profusion of things which pleased them both, were to be found.

Robert had with him his book of Botany, and Agnes had a work on Geology.

They were earnestly conversing, but their tone and manner were not those of lovers, but of friends rather, in whose mental construction the similarity was so great, as to cause a strong vein of sympathy between them.

This, indeed, was the truth.

"I think," said Agnes, "that this must belong to the Tertiary period," producing as she spoke, a piece of curious stone, with bits of a coal-like substance injected into it mosaic-wise.

"And this sandstone must be of the Jurassic time."

"I," said Robert, "am not so well up in lithology as I should like to be, but if you wish any assistance in dissecting and naming the flowers, why, I am at your service, as my botonical studies have been more extensive."

"Then," she said, "I should like to know the sort of flower this is," holding up a little spike with creamy florets threaded about it spirally.

"That is an Orchid, and has a delicate violet fragrance about it, if you notice."

"An Orchid!" she exclaimed delightedly, "why, I thought that they grew only in the tropics."

"Well, then, you have something to learn. There are several of them here in the Northwest. All of the lady-slippers or moccasin flowers are orchids, and then there is a very fine one found generally growing among the phlox of the meadows. It is of a beautiful red-purple color. The one in your hand is the lady's finger orchid."

The girl knew all about the different kinds of golden-rods, of gentians and astors, but was compelled to again ask for information as to the name of a very handsome yellow flower and of some purple spikes with compound leaves.

"The first," said Robert, "is the evening primrose, of which there are several varieties, and the other is amorpha, a very oddly formed little flower, as seen when under the glass of the microscope."

At length she came to a bird's foot violet.

"This," she said, "I found growing near the spot where you said that you and Clipper sometimes set your rabbit traps. Talk of anything being out of season! Why, the prime of this flower was four months ago, and here it is blooming now. This is its aftermath, I suppose. It is, perhaps, like some human lives, who never know any springtime. It is all aftermath with them, or no bloom at all."

"Why, how philosophical you are," said Robert, for a girl of your years. How old are you, Agnes?"

"Just sixteen and two months," she replied, frankly, "but, do you know that I sometimes feel as though I was twenty, and I am sure that I look as much."

"No, that you do not, but you do have a sort of over-worked look about you, for one of your time of life. You do work hard, Agnes?"

He looked at her then more closely than he had ever done before, when he made the discovery that she was not beautiful—not fair looking, even, but, on the contrary, decidedly plain, with her irregular nose, large mouth, sallow complexion and light blue eyes; but her form was elegant and Juno-like in its proportions, and her head, with its mass of chestnut hair, had a classic turn about it, which gave her a distinguished air. He thought of her simile of the violet, and wondered whether her life would be all sterile and blossomless, or whether a glorious aftermath might not, in time, come to her.

"Yes, I work hard. I should not be here to-day, only, you know, that the girls at our establishment are on a strike, and so I am idle by compulsion, as it were. Yet, I do not mind the work,"

she said, bravely, "only I should have liked to go
to school for a term or so longer, if it could have
been done without neglecting those that I love. I
mean my parents, and my brothers and sisters."

"Yes, I know, and there is such a family of you,
too. Let us see, there must be ten, ar'nt there?"

"Just eleven," said the girl, "and if Earl had
lived there would have been a round dozen of us.
To be sure, you remember Earl. Had he lived he
would have been eighteen now, and so good a boy
as he was, and so active, too, would certainly have
been a great strength to poor father, and to all of
us."

"Why, yes, I remember Earl quite well. Don't
you know that I was one of the boys who dragged
him out of the river? I always did believe that
he might have been saved, only for that awkward
Ned Manley. He couldn't swim worth a dead
mud-turtle, and, yet, he foolishly plunged in
ahead of me, and the consequence was that some
of us had to assist him, as well as your brother.
Earl could swim, though. It was an unexpected
blow from a boom log that caused him to go down."

Tears were in the eyes of Agnes at the recital
of the harrowing event, and so Robert changed the
subject at once.

"What do you propose doing, Agnes? Shall
you always work on in this way, for the benefit of
your family, without making an effort for mental
improvement?"

"Yes, my course is determined. I shall just
keep on working, and devote to self-improvement

what few spare moments I can get from my labor, in the belief that this is my duty. By hard effort I may, in time, acquire quite a good deal of learning. There are many examples of self-taught people, who, if they are not able to reach the point upon which they might have rested, under more favored circumstances, have yet the quiet consciousness of a life well spent, along with the elevated pleasure which flows from a knowledge of books. Good books, I mean.

"Well and bravely said, Agnes; "but it is a long lane that has no turn, you know; how will it be about getting married? Some man will carry you off, I am willing to bet, in spite of all your resolutions, or else you are different from the most of girls. They will talk about this and that high notion, and the first thing one knows, farewell to girlhood; and they are off to be married. It seems to be their nature to end in matrimony."

Agnes colored slightly.

At this minute a loud gong-like sound came jarring through the forest stillness, answered by several calls from different directions, and just then, for the first time, young Orme caught sight of the two entranced beings on the opposite side of the water.

"I say, you over there," he cried, "are you asleep, or has the sun baked you into statues? Get up, don't you hear the dinner call," and then he threw his hat into the air, boy fashion; and gave three whoops, so loud that they might have excited envy in the breast of any Sioux or Chippewa

brave who ever walked in these solitudes before
him.

"I'm off," he said, "but not without you, Agnes.
Come, I will assist you to gather up the flowers,
and remember, my girl, that Bobby Orme is
always your friend, and willing to help you all
that he can in the way of books."

Charles and Hetty also arose and ascended the
incline of the bank, their arms interlaced in lover-
like fashion; but before they had gone more than
a few steps along the sylvan path, it was crossed
in front of them by two hunters, dressed in the
suitable garb of sportsmen.

One of them, a tall, dark man, with beetling
brows and piercing black eyes, bowed to Hetty, as
he touched his hat in a sort of military style,
while the smile that passed over his face had a
look of recognition in it.

The young lady returned the salute by a slight
bow of her head, but with no appearance either by
look or manner that she acknowledged anything
of an acquaintance.

"That gentleman seems to have met you before."

"A mere fancy," she replied; but her lover
noticed a slight tremor of her arm, as if it had
startled her somewhat to know that he had noticed
the peculiar look in the face of the stranger.

"I suppose he has met some one who looks
almost as I do and was misled by the likeness."

Then, of a sudden, she commenced a comparison of the present scenery with that of her native
State.

"How tame your scenes are here, when compared with those of my home."

"Do you not think them fine, then?"

"Yes, delightfully so; but I think my preference must go toward the rugged heights of my own state, with its towering, castellated rocks and deeply shaded ravines; where the wild mountain streams come jumping and tumbling down over ferny steps and mossy crags, with a music wild and mystic as the most poetic of temperments might wish. And then, the winter scenes, they are sublime, I can tell you."

"You, who have never been away from this more level land of the west, should, just for once, see the effect of moonlight on the mountain rocks, when they are faced with tier after tier of ice stalactites, glittering in the silver light like a thousand giant gems. I have passed them often while out sleighing."

"Sleighing by moonlight! That is a fine recreation, indeed, in any country; that is, provided the weather be not too cold," said Lennox.

"Well, it is not too cold there, at any rate, and to go softly gliding along over the white way, with nothing to break the frozen stillness, with the looming hills on one side and the ice-bound river and its bank on the other, is an exhilarating affair."

"But I should think there would be danger of falling over that bank into the river."

"Our drivers and our horses are extremely careful there. You see, they are so accustomed to travel

of that sort, that caution has become to them a
kind of second nature."

"Yes, I have read that caution is inherent in
mountain people. It is no doubt engendered by
generations of ancesters, living among such surroundings. The quality must be exercised in
order to protect themselves from the accidents
which otherwise might befall them. But I imagine
that the mineral wealth of those mountains would
have more attractions for me than would the wildness of their outward appearance. I never could
take the pleasure which some persons do among
scenes where the mind, however gratified it may
be, in a poetic point of view, must be pained when
it contemplates the inconvenience suffered by the
inhabitants in climbing over the rough lands and
declivities."

"Look through this opening and you will have
a good view of the river valley and its farms.
There you will see, on their expanse, no such dif-
ficulties to be encountered in drawing from earth
her store of wealth. The farmer of the West is
a very king among men!" he said, proudly.

Now Hetty took no more delight in wildly picturesque views than did her companion; but she
had imagination and elegance of language sufficient to draw a fine picture when she wished to
make it serve a turn in the conversation, as at
present; or, when she wished for effect, to assume
the romantic.

"Yes, I have heard my father say that the mineral stores are almost inexhaustible; and yet they

have recently made heavy draughts upon them.
It is very different now to what it was a few generations ago. Then our people knew little or
nothing about mining, or tempering metal, and so
had to call upon Europe for help. The English
came principally in response with their knowlege,
so that the shafts went down, and the furnaces
went up, in true English style."

"Then I suppose there are a good many of those
people out there. I like the English quite well,
but not well enough to ape their manners, as do
some of our Americans. I, myself, can tell of
some of Albion's blood in my veins, but there is
fully as much of Scotch about me."

"Yes, and I, too, have a good deal of that kind
of lineage among my ancestors, but I suppose it
is just as well for us Yankee folks, as the foreigners call us, indiscriminately, to forget our descent
and remember ourselves as Americans only."

"You are a patriot, my dear ;" and he would like
to have said that, in the time to come, he hoped to
be able to visit her home and friends on the
strength of his tender relations with herself ; but
he left the thought unvoiced, because, he mused,
that perhaps their engagement was too recent to
allow of him speaking in a way so familiar.

Their walk of a quarter of a mile brought them
among the rest of the party, where dinner was
spread, pic-nic fashion, upon cloths on the ground.

"By Jupiter," said Major Stewart, as he and
Lennox reclined upon the grass to enjoy an after
dinner cigar, "what a fine woman that Miss Dud-

ley is, a modern Cleopatra, or a Helen. I should say!"

"Neither," answered Lennox.

He spoke rather shortly. He did not like the comparison at all.

" She is more of a Zenobia, or a Judith, fair to look upon, yet filled with all virtue and wisdom."

The Major shrugged his shoulders.

"Ah, I see," he said, "you are smitten with this paragon, as I have already heard, but why did you make a shift from the gentle little girl with the artistic taste? I thought that you were engaged to her."

Lennox colored slightly. He was annoyed at his talk, and did not like this allusion to his former attentions to Eldie.

"Not quite so far as that. I only thought of her in a brotherly sort of way. Her style hardly suits my fancy. She is too sensitive, too retiring, too much of a dreamer, too much—as we are making comparisons—of an Andromache, or a Cassandria. My ideal of a woman is for one with more dash and spirit about her."

"Well, then, I think you have found your ideal in yon queenly form ; but mind you, boy, that she don't give you cause for jealousy, if you should unite your fortunes. I am older than you, and have seen more of the world, and sometimes women of that sort play the very mischief with men's hearts."

Lennox arose and sauntered off to where Eldie was seated on a knoll, dreamily watching the autumn clouds, as they drifted across the heavens.

She was always looking for cloud-glories, when free from easel and brush. It was a most pleasing recreation for her, and to this habit was due the exquisite skies which attracted the attention of every one who looked upon her pictures.

They spoke together of the beauty of the day, of the charms of the landscape, and he asked her all about her art prospects, and whether she would not like to go abroad to complete her studies.

"Of course," she said, "I should like to go; but you know that Uncle, with nothing but his day's work to depend upon, cannot send me, and it takes all that I earn, past my own expenses, to clothe Camille and keep her at school."

"Yes, poor little Camille."

"You are a good girl, Eldie, and I hope that heaven will reward you and make your life a pleasant one. Here comes John, and I suppose I must resign your company."

He noticed, before he left, that the pale face, with its fine-cut features, looked a trifle more wan than usual; but he little knew of the painful struggle in the girl's heart, as she looked after his retreating form, and thought, within herself, how much dearer his society was to her than that of poor, plain John ever could be."

John was a mere toleration, that was all.

She believed that he loved her. Lennox was irrecoverably gone into the keeping of the eclipsing siren who had come between them, and so she allowed the tide of events to take their own course, and permitted the young farmer's attentions.

Lennox, as he wandered back to the group where Hetty was, ruminated upon the words of Major Stewart.

He did not like to have the woman to whom he had been so recently engaged spoken of in the manner in which he had spoken.

It seemed that the major's opinion of her differed quite a good deal from his own. "But what of that?" he asked himself. "What did it matter as to the opinion of an old fogy like Stewart?"

No beautiful woman would hardly favor him with her love, even though Hetty's plain-faced cousin had accepted him as a suitor.

Toward evening, irregular drifts of cloud began to form along the eastern horizon, and beyond the green serrated line of bluffs to the westward the sky was heavy and dark.

The wind began to surge through the trees with a hollow moan, to curve and purple the water of the lake, and to run swiftly across the rowan of strath and meadow in undulating waves of light and shadow.

"I think we shall have a storm," said weatherwise John, looking westward. "Those clouds have a threatening look, back of all their splendor," for the sun at that moment threw a coloring of rose and amber over their faces.

Accordingly a return home was at once proposed.

They were too late, however.

The rain came pouring down upon them just as they reached the Jaax hovel, and into it they rushed, pell-mell, not waiting for the formality of an invitation.

The owner and his two sons were out looking after the cattle, but his wife, miserable, wrinkled and haggard, was within, and with the assistance of three unkempt girls, was preparing the evening meal.

Unpleasant was the odor from the adjoining stable, made more strong at present by the smell of fried onions and stale cheese as it assailed the nostrils.

As to the condition of the house, it was, as young Orme afterward said, "just too horrible! Why, I had to close my eyes on it all."

But he did not close his eyes, that was a white lie, for, on the contrary, he examined it closely.

"This," he thought, "is the home of the moneyed old wretch who thinks he can lord it over good and respectable Clipper. O, the old curmudgeon! Just look at his filthy and ignorant family! What good can money be to such people? Nothing, only that they may bear the name of having it, and to boast over their betters."

The boy disliked the old German quite as much as did his friend of the rod and line.

The rain was most heavy and the peals of thunder terrific.

Its effects were quite different upon the several members of the party.

Eldie could not look at the play of the lightning without a nervous tremor taking possession of her, while the roar of the thunder she did not mind. She sat, therefore, with eyes closely veiled.

Agnes Flemming enjoyed the electric flash, but could not listen to its noise as it tore its way back to the clouds, so stuffed up both ears with the corners of her handkerchief.

Both Lennox and Hetty were indifferent.

They did not care to get wet, that was all.

The other part of the storm had neither joy nor terror for them, but several others, among them Orme, thought it all magnificiently grand.

Jaax could be heard plainly through the thin partition, stamping and swearing at the horses and cows, which he had driven to cover, and—as a contrast—to his most pious Catholic wife, who was continually making the sign of the cross as she muttered a prayer.

All Christians might do likewise, and in times of danger symbolize that in which they all believe.

The storm at length abated so that they were all able to get home before the darkness of night settled over them, and they could not say otherwise. Then, that the day had been a most enjoyable one to all concerned, and especially to one, at least, of the engaged lovers.

Early the next morning Hetty and her cousin Sarah, were seen by young Orme to come from the picnic grounds where they had been to look for a lost ribbon belonging to Hetty—so she told her companion—but this was an evasion, as what she really looked for was something quite different, and did not become known until after the ermine coat of winter had wrapped tree and bush in its soft fold for the second time since the occurrence.

CHAPTER VI.

The hall of the T—— society was never more elaborately adorned than upon the occasion of the fourth annual ball, given under its auspices, during the holiday week of the year 18—. Many of the city's *elite* were in attendance, for the society was in a most flourishing condition, both socially and financially, composed, as it was, of the most substantial men to be found.

Fashion and gaiety, beauty and wit, had met and joined hands in the endeavor to make as much of an elysium of happiness as it is possible to measure in this mundane sphere.

The great room was one blaze of starry brilliancy, emitted from its electric lights, its atmosphere, mingled with the delicate odor of greenhouse and forest from the festoons of flower and evergreen, while over and among the infinitesimal waves of light and of perfume, swelled the notes of the best orchestra.

"I say, Leonard," said a tall, thin young man with a languid air and an incipient mustache shading his lip, "have you noticed Lennox and the fine-looking girl he had with him?"

"Yes, I noticed them when they first came into the room, but the crowd gathered about them was so great that I could not get a fair look at her. Wilbur, who has had an introduction, says she is grand. None of your optical deceptions, with beauty in the distance, but plainness on a close inspection. There she is facing us now," and down went his hand to his lorgnette, and up it was brought to his eye, and a prolonged stare at the object of conversation was indulged in.

"Ah, she is handsome and no mistake. A lucky fellow, that Lennox seems to be. I wonder where he managed to pick up so fine a prize?"

"Can't say; but this much I can tell you, that when she first encountered my vision, with the full battery of her charms, I was quite shaken in my notions a-la-Darwin. How could it be possible, thought I, for so magnificient a creature to evolve from a protozoa, even through gradations and eons endless."

"You have my concordance there. Even the material part of the human is an unsurmountable block set against the theory. How much more of a barrier than must be the mind and soul of which the body is but the frame, which, grand though it may be, yet is not to be compared with the gem which it encases. I never did believe in Darwin's strange teaching. It may—for a time—sway a certain portion of mankind, but they will eventually fall back on the account of creation as found in the book of ——. Here, take my glass, as I see you have none along with you, and view this newly risen planet to your heart's content. I am an older man than you, and, as a married one, take little interest in the fair sex outside of my own family."

"Oh, you don't eh; well, I do take a great deal of interest in all of them, and especially in yonder one. I vow she is the most beautiful woman that I have ever seen, and how proud that Lennox seems to be of her. By the way, do you know how he manages to get money enough to keep up his style of living?"

"No, I can give you no information on that point."

"I have heard a good many comments lately among his acquaintances in regard to the matter. It is considered odd how he can get on without any visible means of support, as it is well known that he earns nothing, having no trade or profession."

"I think," said his companion, "that, as he is the only son of his widowed mother, that her gratuity, in all likelihood, is his support."

"Pshaw, that's not so. I know all about his mother. She does own a farm of a small size just outside the city limits, and a fine country residence upon it. But what of that? She rents the farm at a thousand a year, which is all of the income that she has, and after living expenses are deducted for themselves and servants, there cannot be much left for Charlie."

"Well, it is a mystery how some people do live, as one may think, upon any fine day in any of our great cities, if he but watch the surging mass of humanity, passing up and down, or standing in groups, as they may list; all of them to get a subsistance out of the hard bosom of old earth. I say, it is wonderful to think about. Here, this peculiar man who, more from incidental causes than any inclination on his part, had been brought into this gay assemblage, went off into a moralizing revery in which social-economy and the future of the masses formed a prominent part.

His young friend filed off in the direction of the magnetic star, whose bright ray had already made her the cynosure.

It was with difficulty that young Hobart, as he was called, could obtain an introduction, but when he did, he made up for the enforced delay which he had undergone by one bold dash, in which he asked for the honor of her hand in the next quadrille; but Hetty had her card written with a half dozen names already, so that, with chagrin, the young man was compelled to place his so far down on the list that he feared the affair would be over before his turn came.

He was as much affected by her loveliness as had been her affianced husband, at first sight; so were a half-score of others, who kept dangling about her.

He thought, as he stroked his downy mustache, and gazed after her willowy form as she gracefully swayed through the delightful mazes of Strauss and of Offenbach, that he would be willing to give the whole of his clerkly salary, of five hundred dollars per year, and himself thrown into the bargain, to be able to call her his own.

Not a great deal of difference. between the margin he had supposed for the support of Lennox and that of himself, from their respective incomes. But, perhaps, he did not consider his manner of living as being in style; or, perhaps, he did not think of himself at all, and only wished to bring forward the disagreeable comments he had heard, as a means of displaying a bit of jealous spite toward his handsome and manly rival, who seemed to be so much in possession of this new beauty.

He employed his time in dancing with some of the less favored of the sex and, indeed, became quite engaged with a bit of a brunette, whose feet seemed formed to follow the terpsichorian god, so lightly did they trip over the floor.

At last his turn came to dance with Hetty. It was one of Wagner's soul-entrancing waltzes, and Hobert thought that the eden of the blessed could not surpass the joy which lighted up his breast, as the fair form of his charmer rested lightly in his arms ; her sea-green dress of silk, with its simple trimmings of white lisse, giving her the look of some nymph from fairyland.

Lennox was out of his usual flow of spirits to-night. He could scarcely say why; it might be caused by that mysterious shadow which some-times comes over us before the approach of evil ; or, it might be, because of the great admiration which his future wife excited in the eyes of his own sex.

Most certainly he was proud of his fiancee, and liked to have her well thought of, but he hardly cared to have so much of a buzz around the woman he would, some day, call by the sacred name of wife.

Why, he asked himself, could not a fair woman devise some means to keep men at a distance, especially those who had no claim upon her friendship.

He might have been answered, that in most cases of the kind, they simply do not wish to keep them off. Too much of vanity in their dear hearts for that ; and, perhaps, the opposite sex would be just as vain had they the chance. They, however, do not have it. Women, as a rule, whatever their f ailings may be, are not fools enough to gather about a man merely because he is handsome. They will, though, wily diplomats that they are, be borne toward him by the metallic attraction of a golden pocket, be he as the ancient Poctolus.

Lennox consoled himself, though, by the thought that Hetty would, in all likelihood, put a stop to any undue notice from others immediately she became a matron, as he had known some fair ones of his acquaintance to have done.

If he felt depressed while in the ball room, he was actually annoyed when he reached the corridor, where he handed his partner into the dressing room, after the dismissal of the dancers.

A note had been thrust into his hand a moment before, and this was its contents:

CHARLES LENNOX:

Call at the office as soon as possible, on to-morrow, December the 27th, as a most distressing case of suicide has occurred, of one of our mortgagees, and a legal investigation as to our business methods may follow.

Yours,

AGNEW & CO.

Hetty, just then coming forward, equipped in her wraps for the street, he hastily crammed it in his pocket, and gave her his arm, and as they stepped onto the stair landing, there, as if waiting for some one, stood the same dark-eyed, beetle-browed man who had met them in the forest as a hunter.

This time he made no sign of recognition, but Lennox noticed that his eyes followed them as they passed out unto the lighted pavement, and toward the sleigh which awaited their attendance. They found, upon meeting the outside air, that it had grown colder and was snowing furiously, but that they need not to mind as they were wrapped in the most comfortable of furs, the sleigh luxurious and the horses of the swiftest ; for, as the youth with the incipient mustache had said, its proprietor had everything in the most elaborate style, and people wondered.

They did not know that the sum of two thousand dollars, which an uncle had kindly given at his valedictory, for he was of the alumni, had only been one-half expended for the purpose for which it was intended—the reading of law—as its recipient had dealt very economically with it, during the two years of his studies.

At the end of these two years, his patron, himself a lawyer, and others of the legal craft, thought

so well of his abilities that he was induced, after
due admittance to the bar, to undertake a case of
of his own.

He met with a failure so complete that it entirely
discouraged him from ever attaining anything in
that direction, and looked upon the years spent in
the acquirement as so much time thrown away.
For awhile he drifted with no income but what
little his mother could spare him.

Then a fortunate thing came to him, if fortunate
that may be called which enables one man, or a
set of men, to see a good time in life at the expense, sometimes the life blood, of others.

An exceedingly lucrative business was about to
be opened in the city by a firm whose members
wished him to add his name to the list along with
his thousand dollars, which he had prudently held
in reserve.

It was a broker's establishment, where money
was loaned at a percentage so enormous that ordinary usury was to it no comparison.

Of course, a sum of money well managed in this
way brought a handsome profit to its owner,
sometimes from the well-to-do man of business,
who sought to relieve himself in a pinch, as the
saying goes, but more frequently from the unfortunate laborer, whom either sickness or want of
employment had driven to the extreme of mort-
gaging his little all, that bread might be obtained
for himself and those dependent upon him, and to
save them from the humiliation of public assistance, or of private charity.

Lennox was induced to join with them, and from that time he had plenty of means at his command, and that, too, with but little bother on his part, as he was not among its working members, so knew but little of their business methods, and cared less, so long as his returns came in all right and his principal was safe.

It is due to the credit of Lennox to say that had he known fully the high-handed means often employed by these men to bring their victims to time, he would at once have withdrawn from so nefarious a way of getting a living, as there was really nothing dishonest in his make-up.

This was the first disagreeable incident which had come to his notice in connection with the firm, and the fact that it had been made to come before him, together with the tone of the note, gave him to understand that the circumstances boded no good to himself and his partners.

Peter, his mother's man-of-all-work, was somewhat out of sorts at the cold time he had experienced while wating about the stable for the ball to close, so gave but curt answers to all interrogitories in regard to his opinion of the roads, and whether he anticipated trouble in getting through the drifts at so late an hour.

No matter, as to his thoughts, favorable or unfavorable, the strong horses stopped at nothing until they were safe at the Desmond door.

Lennox remarked to his companion the fact that a light was burning in the Janneaux cottage as they passed, and wondered what they could be doing up so late.

He did not know that Eldie was so ill that her aunt was under the necessity of giving her nightly attendance, but such was the case.

The almost incessant labor to which she was subject, either in earning means of support, or in assisting about the household duties, was beginning to tell on a constitution naturally delicate; and who can say as to whether the vulgar tales of idle gossip may not have had its share in a secret undermining of the life organs?"

There are natures of so fine an organization that no disturbing influence can be at work without their knowledge.

They are made aware of it without external communication, and the more they are possessed of this tender sensibility, the greater are their sufferings, and the least capable are they of the resistance to their tormentors.

Murder may be committed in different ways.

The hand of the assassin may deal the blow openly, or it may be by more secret methods, among them that one of detraction, with the difference, only, that one alone may be instrumental in the first, but in the second many are apt to partake.

The next day, at the appointed time, Lennox appeared at the office.

There was some little excitement among the number, which had been brought together by a like appeal, but not enough to give an appearance of alarm.

"And so," said a burly looking man, with a coarse, loud voice, "one of our miserable clients has seen fit to shuffle off his carcass by undoing the strings with his own hands, preferring, it would seem, a flight into more airy regions than to longer meet life's sorrows. I don't much blame him, neither. A man with only one leg is but half a man, at best, and when poverty goes along, why life must simply be intolerable. But are we responsible for his rash act?"

"I tinks dot we are not," said a son of Abraham, with a hook nose and a pair of carnation cheeks. "Ve offers our money an de beebles take dere choice."

"It is not our fault dey see fit to borrow at our price. A suicide is von damned man any ways. I no feels peety for de suicide."

" Neither do I," said a squeaky voiced little man, "but I am afraid this affair may create a rumpus in our business, and, perhaps, trouble for all of us. I am sure that I don't know much about the law, but I have my suspicions that an investigation may be able to prove us liable to punishment."

"The law be damned," said the first speaker, with a fierce, lion-like expression. " The law? Why, what is the law? Our method of dealing may be a little crooked, but it is no more unjust than lots, done under the full approval of the code which we have brought with us from a land whose form of government we have thrown off; and they, in turn, got it from the judicial bias of an old churchman, who lived, I can't say how many more than a thousand years ago. He got his inspiration from the laws of Moses, mingled, as it is, with Egyptian superstitions. A fine system to obey, truly, in this age of so-called enlightenment. It seems as though our legal minds are not possessed of sufficient force to throw off the trammels of ancient heathendom and form a set of laws more in consistency with the Christian doctrine. Let them advance if they want better morals."

"I have no fears," said an extremely tall man, as he looked over the heads of the rest.

"They who borrow of us are glad to get the money at any cost, and look upon us as benefactors, no doubt. The widow of this suicide will scarcely say anything about the matter, so far as a thought of investigation goes; as, being a foreigner, she knows nothing of the customs here, and outsiders are not going to interfere with that which does not concern them."

"I don't see that we are doing any crime," said the first speaker, "especially when, as it stands in our fine civilization, as a motto: 'Every one for himself and the devil take the hindermost.' At any rate, though, should anything be mentioned in a troublesome way, remember, all of you, and keep a cautious tongue. Be regular know-nothings, and to hear this little bit of advice is all that you were called here for this morning."

"If any here see fit to visit the wretched widow and her family, with the object of offering to them pecuniary assistance, why, of course, they are at liberty to do so—individual help, I mean. As for my part, I shall not interfere. The household goods were seized and sold, according to due process several days ago, and I suppose they are badly enough off. But it is not my fault."

Among all of the group there was but one man who was sufficiently moved by the sad tale to take upon himself a visit to the abode of misery and death.

That was Lennox.

He received from the speaker the street and number of a house in the northern part of the city, and to it he went.

He was prepared for a scene of destitution, but hardly so much of suffering and sorrow as was presented to his view, when he entered a room on the second floor and saw the family of Walter Bain.

The place was destitute of everything in the way of furniture, except an old cracked stove, in which a poor fire dwindled; four old chairs, two o which served as supports for the pine board upon which lay the remains of the dead.

The man was young yet, not over thirty, with the strong, rugged features and firm looks which mark the Scottish highlander.

The woman answered to the explanation that his visit was one of sympathy, by a flood of tears, and then the peculiar modulations of her native Doric fell upon his ear.

"Oh! the grief of me, sir, I could never tell it ye! I could never begin to tell it ye! Oh! sir, if we

were but back to our old home beyont Inverness!
Why uver did we want to leave it, when we
were so well-to-do in out bit of a sheeling, even if
our eatin was but the oat-meal cake an the garden
kail, and the mulk!"

"But it was all for the learnin to be gotten here
for the bairns, ye see."

"Come lass," he used to say, "let's be off, till the
great land across the sea, where the advantages
are better than here, where puir bodies like our-
sels has to get what knowledge they hae of books
all at night after a hard day's work, and his
practice in figures by cipherin on the clay of the
floor."

"In that grand land all are equal, I am told, an
there are no landlords an bailiffs to press the life
out of ye as they do here."

"An so we crossed the wild water, Walter, the
four bairns and meself, an Oh! sir, would ye
believe it? the great country, so much praised at
home, has given crueler luck an treatment than
we ever knew there, hard and rocky though the
hillsides be."

"We were here but a year an a month, when my
poor Watty, dead now, was run down by a train at
the crossin' on a dark night an the leg taken off
him!"

"What could I do then, but to spend what little
savin's we had to keep him comfortable?"

"It was soon done."

"I left him to the care of the bairns and went
out to wash by the day, for, sez I to mesel, I'll be

a true Scotchwoman and ask help from no one, not
an if I work me hans till the bone!"

"But I fell ill of care an overwork thegither, an
the bairns, too, God bless em, took a fever an in a
short time I was left with three, the biggest being
laid in the grave yard, and times came on so hard
that I was driven to mortgage our bit of goods,
some of them valuable, too, sich as me feather beds
and blankets, and me sheets of home-made Scotch
linen, as ye canna get here for the same price.
For, we reasoned atween us, wi the help of God
we may pull through an the money will give
us our present needs, although it seems a
desperate thing to pay fifteen cents a month on
every dollar used, until we can pay it back
again."

"Well, sir, to shorten my story, we did'nt pull
through, as I could not, with my two hands alone,
keep the enormous interest paid, and live, and so,
according to the binding, our things were taken
from us, an then, as if my sorrow were not great
enough, upon my return from a neighbor's house
on the next day, where I had been to borrow what
little furniture you see here, I found my poor
Watty soaked in his own blude!"

" He was aff i the mind, I an vera sure, else he
could never hae did sic an a deed, and no wonder,
for the puir body was a wantin for the victuals he
should hae had till gie him strength, beside our
great trouble."

Grief overcome the poor woman, and throwing
her apron over her head, she rocked to and fro on

her chair, and sobbed as though her heart would break in her bitter anguish.

Lennox was deeply affected.

He had never before witnessed a scene of poverty and desolation anyway approaching to this, and was appalled to know that a thing of the sort could exist outside of a work of fiction.

He prudently, for his own sake, said nothing of his connection with the loan concern to the woman, and upon his departure pressed upon her the only money his pocket contained, a ten-dollar bill.

" I shall never again draw a cent from the firm," was his mental resolve, as he regained the street; "not if I have to take pick or shovel and earn my living as a day laborer. Only to think that a set of men should be having a good and easy time in life at the expense of so much suffering in others! Why, even the poor children look old and pinched with want!"

He kept his resolve, too, for a week from that day he dissolved partnership, received his invested funds, and withdrew with the secret wish to see in a short time all institutions of the sort abolished.

Two days after his visit an inquest was duly held and a decision given in accordance with the facts of the case.

The funeral took place from the rooms of the Scottish widow; and, on the way to the place of burial, it was compelled to stop at a crossing of streets while another cortege passed by.

The halt was a long one, for the massive, silver-clasped casket, under its pall and plumes was followed by an immense procession of carriages, all filled with friends' of the departed, who had come to offer a show of respect for the dead, and to sympathize with the relatives.

He was a rich man of the community, consequently a respected man, although not known as a Christian or a person of much benevolence.

The poor laborer, it was known in his neighborhood, had been, before his mind became clouded by despair, a most devout follower of the divine word, and in his household the daily chapter and prayer were never forgotten.

The great man had never prayed, or, if he did, it was in the words, "O Lord! give me riches, that I may live at ease and be above my fellow man!"

Each corpse went its way, the one to the fashionable cemetery, where the rich generally find their last bed, there to be covered by a costly mausoleum; to be surrounded by emerald lawns and *parterres* of flowers; by well-kept walks and shady trees.

The other, to a place of more humble pretensions, where, in the potter's field, it will rest among the other poor whose friends but rarely find means to mark the spot of their burial with even a plain slab.

No wonder that the poor, in seeming, neglect their dead.

What do they gain by a visit to their humble mounds?

Surely not consolation, as there can be nothing but sadness come to them, as they witness the contrast between the smooth and ornamented mounds about them, and their own neglected ones with their perennial growth of weeds, for whose care they cannot find time from their daily toil, much less money to buy a head-stone.

The widow Bain did not cause any trouble for the loan society, and they were left to still seize upon the means of delinquent borrowers, and to enjoy their badly gotten gains.

CHAPTER VII.

" Ten beats wiz ze fingers, now strike ze knee, ze elbow, ze forehead."

"Repeat! repeat! repeat!

At each of the three last words, Madame Du Boise clapped her withered little hands and stamped her tiny foot vigorously.

The troupe of Italian gipsies jerked and flirted their tambourines like so many fanciful toys ; the wild rattling notes according well with their not ungraceful movements as they formed into line.

First came the males, with brown pants gaily striped on each side with scarlet or yellow, and fastened at the waist by a crimson sash, a vest of white, and tunic of drab with silver spangles ; the whole contrasting finely with the red kerchief bound gracefully over their jetty locks.

Handsome, stalwart fellows they were, with a well simulated dash of the brigand about them ; and their little commander smiled complacently at her success in the way of her selection of individuals and at the suitableness of their dress, as she elevated her queer parrot nose and her beady black eyes in order to get a better view from her dwarf like dimensions.

She was not so well pleased with the females.

She liked, well enough, their scarlet, black-bound skirts, their tidy feet, and white sleeved chemise, with gold trimmed bodices of black; but their bonnets offended her, and no wonder.

Whoever has seen, elsewhere in the world, anything so *outre* and ungraceful as that worn by the peasantry of the Spanish and Tuscan peninsulas, with its stiff, oblong head-piece of white, and its flowing muslin train reaching below the waist.

"Ze contrast ees not well between olive and white, I zink."

"Bah! fools zat zay are!"

"Vy zay no vare ze red, or ze color de rose."

"But fashing, fashing, zat is ze zing everywhere, and of course it is ze zing in ma belle Italie."

"Go on, you, your dark faces look still darker wiz ze white."

They marched out of their dressing room onto the stage with a regulation swing and beat of their tambourines.

The proscenium was brilliantly lighted, but in the back-ground, drapery and festoons cast a deep shadow, under which clustered tots of children, dressed as wood-nymphs and butterflies, all green and golden.

"For," says the Madame, "peebles want somzing to please ze eye as well ze fancy; somzing to vary from ze common life."

"Zat zay see all time ; here must be vat is different."

Per saltum! and the dance has begun.

The queen and her husband take the lead of the untamed band.

How they whirl, and spring, and sway in true southern style!

How the music swells richly from the tones of piano, clarionet and violincello!

In time the dance is over, and they file off the stage to give room to eight courtly personages who represent France in her ancient glory, with Monsieurs queued and powdered, their coats of scarlet velvet in lace of gold, resting over black knee-breeches, white hose and buckled shoes ; and the Madames no less jaunty, in satin skirts of sable and bodices of maroon, with trussed and puffed trains, and diamonds sprinkled over their heaped up hair.

Their high pitched shoes clicked with their hard heels as they paced through the stately figures of the minuet, and then, with polite gallantry, each beau conducts his lady from view.

An Iceland scene came next.

Here each peasant maid is accompanied by spinning-wheel and distaff, their sombre-hued dresses unrelieved save by the bit of white stomacher and collar, their set square faces by a thick tassle of black, secured at the right ear with a metlic pin.

But their mistress !

Who, but one acquainted with the facts, would expect to find in little barren, far-away Thule, so much grandeur of attire!

Even here, amid all its isolation during the centuries since the sailing Norseman first set foot

upon her rocky soil, has the prevailing social law
had its workings, making serfs of the many,
princes of the few; so that the presiding lady has a
softer and more oval form to her face, a more aristocratic cast of features, and, withal, a more graceful bearing along with the marked difference of
dress.

Her's was the robe of finest silk with argent
braid, a crown of silver upon her head, from
which fell a long veil of finest lace.

A princess, she seemed, as she gave directions
concerning the work at hand, yet with an air quite
free from the spirit of caste when compared with
ways more southward.

Desolate, ocean-sprayed, volcano-racked island!

Its simple fishing and pastoral people are free
from much of the pride and vice of lands more
favored.

The picture from the wintery land is dissolved
to give place to that of a clime almost so bleak,
and a people fully as conserved, for among their
lofty hills and misty lakes modern civilization
makes but slow progression.

They are the clans of the Scottish highlands, in
kilted philibeg, and tartan plaid, with naked knee
and chequered hose, with pinch-purse of hair and
bonnet of blue, they come with the bha of
defiance, their pipes screaming, their notes of
slogan or war-cry, to show their ancient customs.

The loud flourish ends in their national dance,
along with some lassies representing fishwives
and pilse-gatherers from the coast.

Away, then, go the mountain tribe, with their quarrelsome jades, to be followed by the Austrian country-waltz, the men in brown suits and red sashes, with brass-tipped shoes, and vandykes about their necks, and the girls in dresses of blue stuff, with aprons and little crowned caps of white, and bows of ribbon or lace at their throats.

Scenes more oriental are then presented. Of turbaned, curve-slippered Turk, and his close-veiled women in all the gorgeous coloring of their dreamy land, with henna-stained fingers and penciled brows, their soft, languid manners in striking contrast to the band of kerchiefed, grey-clad damsels, who come in their wake with jeweled arms and buskined feet from the caucasus.

And now the fair begins, when all races unite in one grand scale of barter, seated at the tables or hawking their various wares about, with much babble and confusion, until at length they leave the view and the spectacular play ends in a display of draped figures representing the most prominent among the gods and godesses of mythological days.

The curtain drops and the Kirmiss, or national fete, is over.

"A full house," murmers the little Madame, as she peers out upon the dissolving crowd, "and a full house means plenty of money."

Then she sighs a little, as if in regret at her anticipated departure from America.

She will miss the fine income which she has been receiving for her entertainments, and she

wonders whether in all the world there can be
anything which will bring to her the same satisfaction.

Scarcely.

The woman had love enough toward her art for
a successful manipulation of its parts, an eye
skilled in the proper delineation of character, but
over and above all an intense love of gain ruled
supreme and made these but subordinate parts, a
means to an end.

The finest lanscape view, the rarest of rainbow
tinted skies, the sweetest of flowers and the soft-
est of dulcimer notes, had for her no charm only
as they might, through management, be converted
into a money value.

She went back into the rear room where a scene
of confusion met her gaze.

A great number were doffing their stage gear
for that of street wear, and several men were already engaged in a lively brawl.

"Stop ze quarrel, I say!" screams their mistress.

"Vy, if ze new manager see zis he no buy me
out, he go back on ze bargain, sure."

"A pack of ingrates, you, to bring a fuss at ze
last moment!"

"I don't care," says the queen of the gipsies,
"he, there," pointing to one of the French Mon-
seurs, "says that I think too much of Jimmy De-
laney. I will tell him to his teeth that he is a liar,
even if I am married to him."

"Hush, you."

"I won't."

"I shall have you expelled."

"I am going to leave of my own accord, thank you."

"Zat so?"

"Indeed it is."

"A worthless hussy, you are, to go when I promised Monseur Hilton to leave ze troop unbroken."

"Let her go," said her husband.

"I guess the crew can get along without her. They can likely find her betters."

"You speak hard of your wife."

"She deserves it."

"Any woman that has no more respect for herself than to be seen playing cards with a coon, had better leave."

"Vat's a coon?"

"A coon? Why, don't you know that means a nigger."

"Ze sakes alive, vat one talk is dis English; me never learn it!"

"A coon! One dark man a coon, and I never hear ze word before."

"Well, I found her playing casino with a darkey, if that sounds any better, and, besides, I know that she is dead in love with red-headed Jim. I guess I can see as far as I can hear.

"Oh! Oh! Oh!" uttered the actress.

Here she threw herself on the floor as if in a fit, while several of the girls endeavored to raise her upon her feet.

"I wont get up!" she cried. "I won't! I won't! I won't! so you may as well leave me alone. I shall

just lie here to spite him." And she pressed both
hands to the carpet as if to hold herself by it.

"It must be ze hysteria," said the mistress,
"quick, girls, bring me some water."

"Oh! Oh! vat shall I do!"

"Vat, an if ze new manager vill now come! He
vill zink us hard set, I be sure."

"Go away with your water, I am not in a fit, I
am only mad at Will."

"Oh, the villian! to say such mean things about
me, when he knows I meant no harm."

"What if I did play at cards with an innocent
black man, is that so great a wrong? And, as to
being in love with anybody but himself, why, he
knows that is a barefaced lie!"

At that moment two strong arms encompassed
her.

"Do you mean that, May? do you really mean
that you love only me?"

"Of course I do, but I shall not get up from the
floor until you say that you are sorry for what you
have said."

"I am sorry, my May, but how could I help it
when I have been thinking all along that you
were taken with that insolent cuss of a Jim, with
his cock eyes and firey hair."

At this point the discomposed queen arose, the
tears still making little seams of white over her
rogue stained cheeks, a reconciliation between the
two having been accomplished until another spell
of jealousy should occur, and a succession of them
finally end in a divorce court.

Scarcely had Madame Boise been relieved from this grief until another broke out.

Two girls in an obscure corner of the room were wrangling as to the relative merits of their waltzing abilities.

"You can't waltz at all," said one with a willowy figure, "you are too dumpy."

"Yes, but if I am stout and short I know how to give myself a graceful turn, a thing which you seem unable to do, as you just jump about like an Irish jig-dancer."

In this way they had been bantering each other until the dispute had grown into an angry howl.

The nerves of their mistress—already at the highest strain of excitement—lost their balance, and the little woman flew at the two contestants with clenched fists and flashing eyes.

"There! there! there!" she said, pounding them alternately over back and shoulder with all her might, and ended by giving each a slap in the face, "now will you be still, you pests, you jades, you quarrelsome zings!"

"Have you no respect for yourselves, no feelings for me?"

"You know zat ze monsieur say he may be call in ze dressing room afore he go away to-night."

"Come, Agnes," she said, addressing a tall girl who stood as if petrified in the shadow of the curtain, a wondering on-looker at the coarse and curious scene.

"Vy you stand zere so queer, help me to get zese devil's children ready for ze street. I not want Monsieur Hilton to ze zem now."

The girl moved forward in a mechanical sort of way, as she commenced to do all in her power toward assisting in the arrangement of wraps and furs, and in gathering up the scattered parapharnalia and pack them into trunks.

She is our earlier acquaintance, Agnes Flemming.

Thoroughly weary of the wearing and dreary monotony of factory life, as well as to gratify an innate love of travel, for the sake of mental improvement, she had replied to an advertisement offering herself as a sort of waiting-maid and companion to a person going abroad.

This person proved to be Madame Du Boise.

One week in the society of her employer had almost caused her to regret her agreement, and, were it not that a certain dash of resolution beyond the common in her nature always stood in the way of retraction where any of her formed plans were concerned, she would have left her at once to return to her former work at the factory, with its dust and grime, and eternal noise and clatter.

What little she had seen of theatrical life had entirely cured her of the longing, which, along with many young girls, she had indulged in toward the stage; for she perceived that life back of the curtains was altogether different from what it seemed to be upon the boards, in the glare of the footlights, with the fascination of dress, music and the adulation of the crowd. Also, that though good men and women may be, and are, engaged in such work, yet the coarser element is apt to overpower the finer.

She was quite disgusted with it.

There was yet another reason why she was determined to keep her new position, and this was the remuneration she was to receive.

Madame Du Boise had travelled throughout the United States along with her troupe, long enough to bring into her coffers a fortune sufficiently large to have satisfied anyone with a modest ambition.

She was rich, therefore, could afford to give to her waiting woman more than twice the amount of her former wages, outside of traveling expenses.

Fifty dollars a month, with nothing to get out of it, for herself, but her clothing.

How big it seemed to the girl, and what glorious and wonderful castles she built for the future, in which the loved ones at home dwelt in ideal comfort.

Her father, she reasoned, by means of this extra income, would be enabled to go on with his inventions. Her mother would at times, secure to herself the help she so much needed in order to give to her over-worked body some rest; and the childrens' clothes could be made so much more comfortable, to guard them against the bitter blasts of winter.

The vehemence and ardor of her affections, coupled with her youth, caused her imagination to run riot with her judgement, so that the money

which she would send to them was made to ex-
pand until it covered a great deal; in fact, more
than twice the amount could have done; but this
must be forgiven her, as it was but the fruit of her
great and unselfish love for those she was about
to leave behind her.

The two girls were evidently accustomed to the
passionate assaults of their mistress, as they bore
her beats and cuffs with incredible tameness, and,
as if in shame for their conduct, were preparing to
go out as quietly as possible, when the new manager entered.

Madame Du Boise was still in a flurry, with her
face distorted by angry feelings; but the moment
she spied the strange face at the door, the whole
contour of her face changed.

From a sullen and fierce frown, her countenance
became, in a twinkling, one of smiling complais-
ance.

She bowed gently, then extended to him her hand.

To the skilled eye the real heart is seen.

Monsieur Hilton had seen too much of human
nature not to observe the look of hypocrisy upon the sharp, curved features and in the small glittering eyes.

He knew, as if by impression, that a scene had
been taking place.

Most of the girls smirked or giggled as they
were introduced, a few looked at him with modest
reserve, and nearly all were glad of the change;
for they saw in his clear eyes and open brow no
tyrannical master.

An introduction to each member, a few remarks
in regard to their new relations, a critical look at
the faces of the whole assembly, an appointment
for rehersal at a certain hour on the day following,
and Monsieur Hilton bade them good-night, leaving as quietly as he had entered.

Madame Boise was likewise to meet them at the
set time to pay to them all arrears of wages, "for,"
she remarked, "I want the new Monsieur to know
that I am clear of all debts to the company, and
may he always keep you as well paid up."

Then they all felt that, aside from her avarice
and quick, violent temper, there was still something good about the woman.

Agnes kept watching her mistress while in the
car on the way to her home, and, after a long and
careful study of her physiognomy, came to the
conclusion that one might trust her as against
anything dishonorable, likewise that she was
capable of real affection for those who should
rightly engage her attention.

To be sure, the step she was about to take was
rather a daring one, but Agnes was an American
girl, possessed of an American girl's aptitude of
looking upon the best side, both of life and individuals, and, besides, she owned much of native
shrewdness, which gave her the assurance of
being perfectly able to take care of herself, even
though she were going to gay, wicked Paris, of
which she had read a good deal.

She would go along with the Madame when the
time came.

This was her conclusion as she alighted from the car and followed Madame Du Boise into a small cottage, far from the central part of the city, and found herself in a cosy room, warm with a glowing fire of anthracite, and bright with handsome carpet and furniture.

"Take off your zings and lie down awhile on ze sofa. You must be tired out, poor girl," said the shrill, piping voice of the mistress.

"I shall ring for a cup of tea and some hot toast for you to eat before you go to ze bed."

She rang a tiny silver bell, but no response was given.

"Dear me," she said, "I suppose zat stupid Swede have gone out and lefe ze house alone for ze burglars, or else she is asleep after the particular order I give her to be here to receive us when we came."

"I supposed zat you would want some refreshment when ze trying time wiz dose girls sall be over. As for my part, I drink wine, but I guess zat you be not used to it."

Agnes gave a negative answer.

"Yes, I know," went on the little woman, "you Yankee people are—ze most of you—vera temperance, vera much so, indeed, but vot is ze use? Zat's vat I sall like to know. Are you stronger? are you better? are you ze finer here?" putting her finger on her forehead. "I zink not."

"Every one to his way, though, and I shall go myself and make for you ze cup of tea."

She went back into the kitchen and Agnes was left to scrutinize her new surroundings, for, although a week almost had passed since her ntercourse and service with her employer, this was the first time she had set foot within her home.

There was the ordinary plushed-lined chairs, the delicate rocker with its laced back, the center table with cover of gold and purple, the shining plated stove, the heavy draping of the windows, a lambrequined shelf, upon which a tiny clock ticked away the minutes and chimed away the hours.

In one corner of the room a gilt cage held a drowsy parrot, and upon the wall a solitary picture was hung.

This picture attracted her attention.

It was the one which had been bought by the strange woman out on the Lyndale road.

This cottage she knew was on Lyndale, and the woman must have been Madame Du Boise, then, who had patronized her friend.

While engaged in a scrutiny of it the sleeping parrot awoke and at once commenced a tirade of abuse in its stereotyped manner of words.

"Go out! go out! nasty thing! nasty thing!"

It kept on at the repetition, until its mistress appeared with the tea and toast, when its scolding song was changed to one of pleading.

"Polly wants her tea, Polly wants her tea," it cried, until its voice was stilled by some toast being thrust between the bars.

"An imprudent sauce-box, zat," says Madame, "one who rules me and all about the place."

"Now eat your bite and drink your tea, Agnes, after which you must retire, as it is getting quite late, eleven and more; but then you need not arise too early in ze morning, take your nap out and I shall see zat ze breakfast is kept for you."

"I was just observing the picture yonder," said Agnes, looking to the wall. "Do you know that the artist is a friend of mine?"

"Is it so?" asked the owner a little surprised.

"Yes, she is a near neighbor to me when I am at home, and her name is Janneaux, Eldie Janneaux."

"Why, zat is one French name! it is to be sure."

"Yes, it is French, and Eldie is of French extraction, and some say that she has Indian about her, too; but I cannot say whether the last is true. At any rate she is a dear, good girl, whom everybody loves."

Madame Du Boise looked at her in a queer sort of way.

"And how long ago came ze people from France? I mean her people."

Oh, I am not able to say as to that. They are Canadian-French, I believe, and most of them there are of old stock, dating their foreign ancestry back to three or four generations, and even more. They are mostly thoroughly Americanized."

"I saw ze picture at ze art rooms, and finding out where ze owner lived, I drove over and bought it. I paid ze money to a man and he brought it out to me as I stay in my carriage."

"That must have been Eldie's uncle."

"I got ze painting, because ze little boy on ze bank of flowers is so like one boy I once did know."

Then, as if to change the conversation, she began to scold the bird for dropping crumbs upon the carpet, after which she offered to show the girl to her chamber.

"Go out! go out! nasty thing! nasty thing!" assailed their ears as they ascended the stairs, and Agnes wondered whether the noisy chatterer was to be an accompaniment across the ocean, and thought that her companion seemed to have much less control over the bird than she did over the members of the theatrical troupe.

The next day was spent by Madame Du Boise in meeting her former pupils in the art mimetic, and to attending to some shopping affairs preparatory to her journey; and by Agnes in paying a farewell visit to her home and acquaintances.

There was the usual amount of sadness displayed by her parents when the oldest, the best loved child of a family is about to branch out into the world for the first time, and to be thrust beyond the customary home influences.

Had Mr. and Mrs. Flemming consulted their own feelings they never could have consented for her to leave their care for that of a total stranger.

To have her leave her own land for one beyond the seas, even though the time promised to be short; but the poor have not the ordering of their lives.

They thought of the possible advantages which might fall to their child in her new relations, of the difference in their incomes, along with her own inclinations, which they felt to be proper enough.

Then there was the unbound faith which they had in this pure, strong girl of theirs; faith that insured her to them to hold good her integrity in all emergencies.

She bade them a tearful farewell, with the promise that not more than a year should pass before her return to her native land and to her loved ones.

The furniture of the cottage was soon disposed of, all but the painting, and, in accordance with her half expectation and to her annoyance, the bird and the cage, the last to be carried by Agnes herself and to fall under her particular supervision.

The picture was packed into one of Madam's trunks, and it was noticeable what very great care she took of it; at one time being surprised by Agnes while in the act of pressing her lips upon that part of the canvas where the boy was represented!

She made no explanation of the movement other than to say that it was so cunning a portrait that it quite entranced her, but the listener considered the proceeding as singular, at least.

In due time they reached the great steamer which was about to launch from out the harbor of New York Bay, without any unusual occurrence, except that Agnes mistook the parlor of the steamer which was to carry them from Hoboken across the channel to their starting point, for the waiting room of the railway station; and thought the vessel a long while in coming for them; when, to her surprise, she was told that she had been sailing for some time; was, in fact, almost in the great metropolis!

She was, however, not the first who has labored under the like false impression of surroundings at the same point.

The grand ocean!

How delighted the mid-land born girl was the first time she caught sight of its broad, glittering expanse; and how refreshing was its breeze to her after a sojourn of a day and half in New York.

Once fairly out of land sight, in the freshness of a spring morning, it seemed to her like the commencement of a journey to some other world than this, so strange was the new sensation; a sensation which for hours kept her from even thinking of the home and friends she was leaving behind.

Indeed, throughout the entire run of thirteen days her principal place was upon the deck, where, among other passengers, she walked up and down engaged in admiration of the water-kingdom, with its gently undulating surface, green, blue, or bronzed by the sun's rays, or else sitting in a corner absorbed by her books.

She was fortunate enough to escape sea-sickness, but not so the little Madame, for she was ill quite a good deal of the time, but thoughtfully made as little trouble as possible, so that Agnes was not often called away from her pleasant place in the air and sunlight, to the less cheering one of the cabin.

But the bird had no such lenient inclinations toward her.

His wants must be attended, otherwise he would make it known by the most terrific screams, uttered along with his usual string of abuse.

It was, while attending to him one day, in a nook of the deck, where she had deposited him among some rope coils and boxes, that she made the acquaintance of an English ornithologist, Alfred Rae.

He was and elderly man of fifty, or near to sixty, perhaps, with iron-grey hair and whiskers.

He introduced himself, with the apology that his great love for birds always induced him to speak to any person who had one in charge.

Then he told her all about the peculiarities of the family to which this bird belonged, taking Polly from the cage as he talked, and caressing him as tenderly as he would have done a child.

He was also something of a philosopher, as she found during their talks together, and spoke one day of different authors of his, Oken, Hegel, Spencer.

His was the Hegelian method.

"I believe with the great German," he said, "that to philosophize is to rethink the great thought of creation for all nature, all of the human mind is but what God has made it."

He seemed glad to have a listener to his abstract thought, for—parenthetically, it may be said—that they were not over plenty, so that even though it were but this unletterd girl, who listened to him with wonder and admiration for his knowledge; although the most of his words were Greek to her, who knew little beyond the elementary books, still his scientific discourse gave her a glimpse into the wonders of nature and of nature's philosophy, as he took pains to explain it.

He proved to her a pleasant companion, until the arival of the steamer at Havre, whence he took his departure for a science congress to be held somewhere in Germany.

They took railway from Havre to Paris, arriving there at four in the afternoon, just as the declining sun was lighting it up with a radiance of roseate glory; and Agnes thought the sight fine indeed, but her companion was entranced almost beyond herself with delight upon the fair and busy scenes which met her gaze.

She had been from it many years, and yet all this time, with the advent of new places and views, had not one whit of power to abate her love for this, her early home.

"Paris! my Paris!" she exclaimed with the pronunciation peculiar to her people, and in all the nervous excitement belonging to the race, "how delightful to be once more upon your streets!" Then her address died away in a phrase or two of French.

This is true, that whatever the faults of the French Capital may be, no inhabitant of another city has the love for his home that the Parisian feels for his.

To the stranger it is a place rich in historical associations, of early educational facilities and antique synods, also a place of siege, of war, of tumult, and red-handed injustice. But to the native, it is Paris, the queen of the Seine, the home of high-blooded nobles, and plebean, the garden of beauty and of pleasure; Paris, the golden!

They drove to a house in the Rue de l'Orme, where the Madame had, by dispatch from Havre, engaged rooms and boarding for them, and here they found rest from the fatigue of their journey, the spot being quiet and retired.

A few days after she bought a snug little residence not far from the Champs Elysees, for, as if to, in a manner, regain some of the pleasure she had lost away from her beloved soil, she sought the city's most beautiful part, even though it caused her to draw heavily upon her money pile.

Afterwards came the furnishing, which was done in good taste. The securing of a servant to attend to domestic affairs, of a porter to do the errands, keep the little garden with its one tree of St. Katherin's pears in order, and the grass of the little yard at the front neatly cut, also to take charge of the pony and pheaton, which she purchased along with the dwelling.

In this cosy nest the little woman expected to stay until the time when—in all likelihood—she would rent it for a season, while she made a second trip to America, where, by means of her former profession, she might again fill her purse.

She had meant to return at the time of her leaving, and it was this idea that caused her to advertise for a traveling friend while there, as she thought by a continual contact with an English-speaking person to improve in her knowledge of the language by that time.

Agnes was delighted with her quarters.

Her mistress increased in kindness to her daily, her duties were not severe, her wages were paid with exact regularity at the end of each month; the reception of her money checks, duly chronicled, in the letters received from her home together with an account of the most gratifing results to the family through the bounty received.

Twice a week she went along with Madame Du Boise to the grand theatre Royale, where, although she could not understand the language of the plays, yet she was charmed by the soul-thrilling music of the fine orchestra, the gayly dressed men and women, the handsome building and rich scenic display.

Sometimes they attended the different art galleries, one of whose pictures her companion was so well acquainted with that she knew nearly all of the history connected with them, of how the painter of this one was an extremely poor man, one of the lowest among the peasant class. Slowly he had arisen by the force of his own merit, until at last he had reached the highest niche of his profession, and died rich and respected.

Of the next, which was painted by a Genoese who was compelled to flee from his native land and to find a refuge in France, all on account of political complications—of another, the wife of a nobleman, la Comptesse La Noir, who had been beheaded by Murat.

Then came the tale of one which had been made by a shoemaker artist, who was compelled to ply his trade as a means of subsistance in the dark days preceeding the outbreak of the revolution, when artisan and labor were ground to the very dust by an overreaching aristocracy, along with a corrupt government. Of how his genius struggled against all odds with a force which could not be baffled, causing, by it pressure, time to be found to devote to its imparative demands—of how he toiled years upon years without recognition, until at last, at the age of seventy, he produced this, his master piece, which brought him both fame and riches. But the rebound from his woful indigence and humility to one of affluence and honor was so great that he died in a short time of the effect, it would seem—died of overjoy.

Agnes thought that of all the pathetic stories connected with them, this was the most pitiful.

To think that anyone should, Sysiphus-like, have the stone of fate to roll continually back upon them through such an age of years, and when at length he did succeed in keeping it off to die of the very success of the effort!

She dearly loved to roam about in view of the works of these great people, and to listen to the short biographies of them given by one who seemed to have acquired quite a good deal of picture lore in her life time, relating it with great fluency as it recurred to her memory.

On fine days they rode through the Champs Elysees, along the shaded boulevards, or visited the vicinity of the Louvre or of the Truilleries, and upon Sundays went to the church of Notre Dame, to hear the rich notes of the organ in Gounod's Messe Solemnelle, or to listen to the deeply intoned chanting of people and surpliced choir.

Agnes commenced a study of the language of the country into which she had so suddenly been brought.

She wished to learn it for her own sake and also to please Madame Du Boise, who wanted her to learn it, "if," as she said, "for no other reason than that she might, among her other duties, teach it to Polly, as it would be so cunning in him to be able to chatter his limited phrases in her own tongue!

Madame Du Boise seemed to have but few acquaintances in the city.

Either her former friends had all taken their departure during her absence, or else she had never had any, and what few did recognize her in doors or on the street all seemed to be of a rather shabby class, so that Agnes inferred that the

little woman with the eccentric—and, at times—
coarse manners, must have in her earlier days
belonged to the ordinary class of work-women, or
grisettes, as they are termed among the Parisians.

She never mentioned her past life except once,
and that was when she was driving past an old
and dingy factory of some sort, when she said, "I
worked here when a young woman of twenty,"
but as she was now fifty, that period carried her
back thirty years, and proved that although Paris
might not be her native soil, it had long been
her place of abode, also any friends she then had
might have died or left the place.

At any rate the possibilities of Agnes seeing
much of the social life of the gay capital seemed
to be limited in the extreme, and that the Madame,
appearing to realize this, was determined that the
young American should, at least, see some of the
natural beauties of that part of Europe which
was contiguous, and as this would likewise be of
the most striking portion to one of her temper-
ment, it would leave a lasting impression upon her
mind as a happy remembrance of her trip abroad
in years to come.

So she reasoned, and in order to bring about
this effect upon one whom she began to love as a
daughter almost, she organized the plan of first, a
journey up the Rhine, with a sojourn among
the Alps, and then a run into Italy.

They left Paris the middle of July and was soon
in the land of gothic splendor, on board of one of
the lazy steamers which ply the blue waters of

the far-famed and enchanting river of the north; with its prospective castles towering high on crag or knoll, its drowsy old towns, sheltered close under the vine-clad hills, its quaintly dressed and brusque mannered men and women, and its buildings of peaks and gables, while over all the yellow shower of the summer sun shedding its pale glow on rock and ruin, meadow and ravine, with such a spirit of sleep in its misty depths that all life seemed to have left the place so quiet was the scene.

This quiet intensified as the night shades began to lengthen along the river and to creep over tower and hill, tinging the water with a deeper purple, and the blue of the sky with a darker hue.

Then the little steamer pulled up for the night at a village which seemed to be possesed by extremely cold-blooded inhabitants, as they were put to bed upon feathers piled so high that they were under the necessity of mounting upon chairs in order to reach their downy depths; and where everything was so scrupulously neat and clean that the aroma from the kitchen reminded them of eating, with pleasure. No fear of dirt here.

In the morning they found that the business of the place was carried on chiefly by short-petticoated and tight bodiced women with panniered donkeys, and girls with boquets of cultivated flowers, one of whom, with a not ungraceful air presented a bunch to Agnes, with "liebmassen und veilchen der shone franleiu," as a gift, apparently, but she knew, or divined at least, that money was expected, and accordingly dropped a sou or two in her hand in return for it.

Trade was mostly between the venders and the bargemen along the river. The last bought food supplies or the few passengers who happened to stop occasionally for a night's lodging, or a few days rest, brought them money enough to keep up a knowledge of its appearance at least.

In time they passed the Drachen Fels, or Giant's rocks, the seat of the Lorlie, or invulnerable fairy, whose siren song of old was wont to lure unwary boatmen upon the rocks at her feet, and so to ruin; with all the other charmful spots which are usually pointed out to tourists along the rugged banks of the picturesque stream.

After a week or more spent in this way they left for the Swiss Alps, where they ensconced themselves in a chalet in the very shadow of the Wetterhorn.

Here they engaged a guide who spoke both German and French to pilot them about the vicinity.

This was well enough, as he proved both skillful in his profession and well posted in all legends of the place, the only drawback being that Madame Du Boise was obliged to translate all that he said into English for the benefit of Agnes.

Only one of these she thought of sufficient importance to explain in full, of thrilling wildness and peculiar adaptation to the surroundings it was, and interwoven with it a love romance so strange that it is not to be wondered at that the

guide—by the extra force he put upon its narra-
tion—considered it as among the choicest of the
stories ever to be found where humanity has lived
its fitful day and sang of life. It ran in this
fashion:

Upon a green knoll high up among the mountains it was the custom in days past to hold at
times the festivals of the village folks, so pleasant
was its situation and so smooth its sward for the
feet of merry dancers.

Wilhelm and Pauline were betrothed lovers.

Here, among others, they came to celebrate the
flower-feast or Spring festival, which was held
annually the first of May; Wilhelm in all his
peasant strength and blooming manhood; Pauline, fair and shy as a violet, in her robe of white,
her golden hair bound by wreaths of forget-me-
not, rivals for the blue of her eyes, while her manners were as fresh and as charming as the month
itself.

Both were as happy as it is possible for young
hearts to be without the least presentiment of evil
to cast its gloom about them, or to warn them of
the strange event which was to separate them
forever.

Pauline had another lover, one, however, to whom
she gave no encouragement, but whose persist-
ance in his suit was unbounded and untiring.

His name was Gaspard Bach.

Along with the rest he came to the fete to enjoy
himself and to have, if possible, one dance at least
with the beloved of his heart.

His request was granted, not, however, without a protest from Wilhelm, who was loth to see his bonnie bride in the arms of his rival, but this protest was unheeded by the laughing girl, who could see no harm in a lively waltz along with him more than another, so away they whirled among the giddy throng, crushing the wild flowers, with which the ground was strewn beneath their feet, dancing on and on, for a long time and in such wild glee that Wilhelm had barely time to catch what he imagined to be an imploring look from the girl as she passed him for the twentieth time, as if she wished to be released from the strong embrace of her companion.

He determined that when they should again come around after their tour of the great circle, he would interfere in Pauline's behalf, as they had already out-danced all on the ground and were the soul respondents to the music.

A queer and fearful fancy came to him, as he gazed after them, and noted the strange, fierce look on the face of Jaspard, along with the pale, agonized one on that of Pauline.

Great God, the man was mad! He would not release her from his grasp!

His discovery came too late!

At the side opposite to him, some twenty-five yards distant, the knoll was protected from the steep declivity overlooking the valley below by a high balustrade, without opening or gate at any point, but as the two dancers, with lightning rapidity neared its middle part, it seemed to open as if by magic and they disappeared among the heavy fir trees which fringed the summit behind it!

With a cry Wilhelm started for the point followed by a crowd of young people, several of whom, along with himself, had noticed their odd looks and the singular exit back of the enclosure.

There was no trace of them to be found, and nothing to indicate the transpiration of the startling event, except three pickets lying upon the ground, as if they had fallen away for them at some talismanic word.

They all hurried to the mountain path leading down among the rocks, half expecting, yet dreading, to find their mangled remains.

Nothing of them was found!

Jaspard and Pauline were never either seen or heard of again.

A few thought the affair was a plan between them, and that a secret path, known only to Jasperd, had led them off in safety, and that in some distant land they shared each the other's love.

Others, of a more superstitious cast, supposed the man to have belonged to the evil one, and, therefore to have danced away to the infernal regions, bearing the fair bride along with him.

Wilhelm, though, was confident that their forms lay bleaching upon one of the many crags which jutted out from the surface of the rocky height, and where no eye but that of the eagle or vulture ever saw; and, underneath them, he was often found with his rude harp playing some sad strain, as if to the departed soul of his darling, for whose sake he remained unmarried until the day of death.

His belief was generally shared, so that the lonely mountain pass grew to have a name of being haunted, the beautifully rounded hill top was no longer used as a place of merry-making and to this day, the guide said, the people of the neighborhood avoid it by night when the phantom reelers may be seen flying across the face of the cliff, Jaspard in his suit of brown, with a white kerchief knotted at his throat, and Pauline in her misty dress of white, with her ribbons floating about her, just as they appeared when last seen."

From there they went to the lake of Lucerne, and spent a few days gliding about on its calm waters, where the sky or flitting cloud is for ever mirrored, and where at night the golden moon from her own misty ocean finds a fitting background to reflect her fair form.

Beautiful Lucerne!

Agnes never forgot the elevating influence of its soft, poetic beauty, nor the more busy scenes about Geneva to which they went from there, and thence across to Mount Blanc, through the Grand Alps, and back toward their starting point.

If to the native and the stranger Paris is a gem, so also are its environs; with vale and champaign, decked as it is - with richly cultivated gardens, emerald fields, charming villas, and superb chateaus.

Versailles, through which they passed, brought
to the mind of the young American all the mem-
ories of a time when the royally crowned heads of
Europe met to assist in the political baptism, and
thereby give assent to the birth of the new
government that had dawned so suddenly upon
the world. St. Cloud, which they took in circui-
tously, paid for the extra trouble by its lonely
grandeur, and the mellowed recollections which
it brought of the haughty Emperor, Napoleon the
First, where, with his Austrian wife, he passed
the time surrounded by his Imperial courtiers;
with no shade allowed to trespass upon the peace
of his imperturable nature from the outer world;
unless it might be, that the iron heart in his
bosom could not always keep off the sadly beautiful and ever pleading eyes of that other and first
wedded love, his much wronged Josephine.

From here they reached Ville d' Avray, a lovely
little place resting under the shadow of the Boise
de Marley, where the Madame proposed spending a few of the Autumn months along with a
first cousin of her's, who resided here.

Her relative, who, like herself, was middle-aged,
received her with joy as in a race like that of
theirs, whose family tree had borne but little
fruit and that mostly too frail to long survive
their birth, relatives were scarce.

What few there were had quite an appreciation
for one another. With a more extensive following
of blood the feeling between them might have
been somewhat different.

These two had survived the shocks and wrecks
of time, with no more of a showing for the years
in the face of Madame Du Boise than that already
described; and no more on that of her cousin than
was indicated by a few white streaks here and
there among the black of her hair, and a pucker
of crows feet beneath her eyes. On the left cheek
quite a large protuberance, in the shape of a wart,
had made its appearance since they last met.

Warts are not by any means a sign of age, but,
coming as this did with her ripening years, it
seemed to be in her case of one of the dreaded
prognosticators, and, as from its centre sprang
four or five hairs of a third of an inch in length,
it gave to her face a grotesque look, indeed, especially as the hairs were never either extracted or
sheared, under the impression, no doubt, that, like
gray hairs, the more they were eradicated the
more they would come.

But this beauty destroying visitor served an end.

Madame L'hommechapeau, she was called, by
that conception of courtesy peculiar to the French,
who consider the title of Madame much more
respectable for ladies past a certain age, than the
same syllables with a "selle" appended.

L'hommechapeau, which, under the pen of the
translator would stand out as "the man's hat,"
was both peculiar and long to speak, so that many
persons not well acquainted with her, spoke of
her as "the woman with the bearded wart."

It was necessary that she be well known
by some name, as she was quite a prominent

person in a business point of view, being the best
maker of cheese and of butter in the village. Brie
and Mananta cheese could hold no parity; while
she held—and so did her neighbors—that the
Rochefort and Chombert varieties, though coming a little nearer to the standard, were abominable in comparison.

She had a lovely home on the outskirts of the
village, say a fourth of a league from its border,
just far enough away to be somewhat protected
from the depredations of vagrant urchins, or mischievous school children, who, otherwise, might
cast an evil eye toward· her small orchard, where
the purple gooseberries and scarlet cherries
tempted the robins in midsummer, and the red
and russet apples, the golden pears and the yellow
quinces, showing like royal jewels among the
green of the leaves, rivalled the perfection of form
and color in the work of the most eiquisite of
artists.

Then there were the nut trees.

A great wealth was in the food producing
qualities of those garden giants.

Many a meal was made from the kernal of the
rich brown chestnut, either boiled or roasted, and
the walnuts served as a desert, cheap because
home raised.

Commonly her household retinue of two servants for domestic use and her two workmen
about the place fared plainly enough, on thickened
milk, rye bread, cheese and a few vegetables; but
she made up for this on Sundays, holidays, or

when honored by a visit from friends, or, as at present, a relative.

At such times the long oaken table in the flag-paved kitchen with its dressing of pewter plates and horn spoons, was deserted for the polished mahogany one on its shinning casters in the tidy dining room, with its waxed floor and curtained windows.

The finest of linen cloths was laid, the old heir-looms of china, of glass, and of silver were brought forward in the way of dishes, and then their filling process commenced.

Ma foi! as her countrymen would say, what a cook was she!

How appetizing the odor which arose from well scoured pot, kettle and pan, as she lifted the savory mess of meat, fish and fowl from each, and how fragrant was the steam which came from tart, pie and pudding. And what cakes!

Could Berlin or Vienna produce their equal?

Or was the table of that redoubtable sailor, Sinbad, ever graced with better?

Then there were the anchovies, the truffles, the olives and the foigras, the Carlsbad waters and the fruits!

Seville oranges, she declared to be the best in the world, and grapes from sunny Gallic slopes the only ones for her, and when she must have foreign fruits, why, then give her those of Weisbaden or of Leghorn.

The scene from the high-pitched dormer windows of the gothic house was in itself a poem of quiet pastoral beauty, with its long sweep of hills running westward and Parisward, or to the east. The emerald meadows and fields studded by clusters of oak and of linden, while to the front of the building the lawn fell in a slope to a willow-fringed stream, separating it from the shining turnpike.

At the side of the house facing the east was the garden of vegetables and flowers. Here, in the early spring, amidst the blustering winds of March, the white and purple crocus pushed its way through the cold dark soil of the earth, along with its sister—the pasque flower of France—the beautiful, wool-stockinged, lavender-hued prairie flower, of America, whose blooms the children so love to gather. Then a little later the yellow jonquils, the white star flowers, the grape hyacinth, with its tiny globes of blue, the daffodil and polyanthus, the peonies, the lillies, the lilacs, syringas and snow-balls; all keeping up their prime until they meet the dahlias, hollyhocks and chrysanthemums of the more mature months.

Yet there were the beds of seedlings, which in their flush, had been one mass and tangle of color, fair and varied as ever the golden-footed Iris pressed as she skimmed along her rainbow stair.

But now, in October, the most of the flowers showed but faded remnants of their beauty in a few late pansies, some lark spurs, and Agnes' favorite flower, the little star-like elisia sunk in modest retirement among its mossy leaves; and these, even, wore a desolated look among the dead and withered surroundings and overshadowed by the evergreen foliage of the myrtle, the holly and the fir.

Not more than the space of two hundred yards away was the home of a modern Scheherazade, so far as the story-telling ability was concerned.

She, a girl of twenty-six, wrote for nearly all of the literary papers of Paris; one in Marseilles, another at Bordeaux, besides making contributions for a magazine. Low, indeed, was the price of her works.

Ten pence a column was the usual remuneration, but by dint of hard labor, she managed to to support herself and her widowed mother quite comfortably.

Marie, Madame L'hommechapeau's maid from Normandy, in her white cap and sabots, was the gossip who told Agnes all this in the broken English which she had picked up while at service in the Hotel 'd Anglaise, Paris.

Agnes was much interested in the story of the youthful literateur, and wished very much for a closer acquaintance, but it ended where it commenced, by a sight of Adele, from her chamber window as she wal ed forward and back, under the linden trees in front of her dwelling with her gold brown hair brushed tightly back from her pale temples, in a very unfashionable way.

At this place Agnes for the first time met for herself a lover.

This was Guillaume, the sprightly, dark-hued young gardener, who took care of the grounds.

He was extremely kind in his bearing toward
her, culling the finest apples, the sweetest pears,
and forming the most delicate of boquets for her
benefit.

After the evening work was done, he would take
her, along with Marie, to ride behind his donkey,
in a rickety farm-cart, over the graveled way,
under the thick leaves of the rowan trees, with
their clusters of berries shining like great sparks
of fire; over the little wooden bridge that spanned
the stream with the milky-green of the ivy leaves
covering its ancient butresses; out onto the shining highway, where the tall lombardies skirting
its sides, cast long shadows away from the falling
sun—like living creatures who flee the dying.

Here the air was heavy with the perfume of
orchards and the scent of meadows, both lately
stripped of the last mantle of autumn grass.

Ceres, with her crown of silver, was surely most
favorable to this part of the land of St. Louis, or
else so many happy peasant homes, rich in life's
comforts, could not look out from so many bowery
scenes as greeted their sight, when they rode
along by bits of woodland, or open strath, where
the thrush was singing its late song, and the
blackbird was swinging to the music of his screaming notes among the stiff water-flags and reeds.

And the sky!

How it circled around the horizon a great concave of ethereal blue, and as night came on how
the Pleadies twinkled and flashed like electric
lights, seen through a haze, and how Orion looked

down as an armoured giant, while Arcturus in the
north, the constellation of Ursamajor, and the
lode star vied one another in diamond-like brilliancy with Vesper or the star of the evening, as
she gracefully hung above the sable of the distant
hills, all with the same form that they were to the
eyes of those loved ones, so far away in her western home!

The time came when Madame Du Boise found it
expedient to make an end to her cousinly visit,
therefore when November, with its chilling winds,
was beginning to scatter the scarlet and yellow
leaves into drifts and eddies over the dark ground
and a necklace of icy jewels had lightly strung
itself along the water's edge, fair and delicate as
the ornaments of a queen; they left the thrifty
homestead beyond V'lle de Varley, and took their
way back to the metropolis, and Guillaume, the
gardener, looked after them as the vehicle which
bore them rolled away, a gloom upon his face and
a sorrowful look in his eyes.

She was the only woman he as yet had loved,
and she had given him no token that his passion
was returned, nor thrown out any hopes of their
ever meeting again. Would he ever forget this
first sweet dream of youth?

Of course he would, like the majority of his
kind, take to himself a wife, in all likelihood one
more suited to his tastes and habits of life than
Agnes could have been, but throughout his course
there would come times when a shadow would
fall across his memory, and a hand invisible as

the zephyr which stirs the eolian lute-strings to
music would vibrate the chords of his heart to a
saddened strain; for first love is never altogether
forgotten, however its influence may be deadened.
They reached the borders of Paris in safety, but
here one of those accidents occurred which, however commonplace they may be, constitute such
an element in the chain of one's life, that they
seem to be a determined agent, to work out the
plans of existence.

It came about all through the carelessness of
a luggage-man, who failed to put the great trunks
of the Madame in a proper position upon the
top of the hack, which they had engaged to take
them to their quarters. In consequence of this
event of care it fell back to the pavement
with so great a force that its two plethoric
sides burst open, throwing out all it contained
by the movement in a confused mass at its owner's feet.

Among dresses, laces, scarfs, feathers and other
paraphernalia of the female toilet, the picture also
made its appearance.

Madame began to scold furiously in French,
calling the unlucky workman all sorts of names
appropriate to his act of stupidity, but as soon as
she caught sight of the picture her attention was
so attracted, that he escaped the remainder of her
tongue's vituperation, much to his relief.

"*Mon cher petit garçon,*" she exclaimed
with feeling as she continuously withdrew it, all
unhurt, from the pile, and in seeming forgetful-

ness of her surroundings, pressed kiss of kisses
upon the surface of the cold canvass.

An elderly gentleman who happened to be passing at the time, stopped a moment to look at the
demolished trunks and the wreckage, when he
chanced to hear the words and to note her
conduct.

It caused him to give a more scrutinizing gaze
than he might otherwise have done toward her
and the picture, and as soon as his eyes rested
upon the latter, a strange and wondering look
came into them. He pressed forward among the
small knot of bystanders, who had gathered
around the scene, and, in his own language,
begged leave for a closer view of that which she
seemed to hold so dear.

She could not well refuse a request so civil,
although she considered his curiosity in the matter
but little less than an unwarranted intrusion.

She cast an uneasy glance towards his tall
figure, as he stood contemplating the painting in
her hands.

"May I be allowed to ask," he questioned in
tones of refined modulation, "whose child was the
original of this and by what means you came
by it?"

Madame flushed scarlet with anger, but she
subdued her emotion sufficiently to reply to his
question.

"Monsieur, I am not able to tell you whose the
boy may have been, but certainly I can tell you
where, and of whom I bought it.

"From America it comes, and it is the work of a friend of the young girl here, pointing to Agnes, but I have forgotten her name."

"Does she speak French?" he asked.

"But indifferently, that is quite unintelligibly. You could not understand her jargon. These Americans never can be made to speak our grand speech, so that one can know what they are saying."

She did not care to have him pry any more into her affairs than he had already done, therefore she wished to thwart him in any attempt at a conversation with her serving-maid; somewhat understanding the dialogue between them and not knowing of the conservative feeling of her mistress, said innocently, "The name of the artist is Eldie Jannaux."

"Jannaux," he repeated after her, musingly, with his eyes to the ground, "Jannaux, I have heard that name before. It is decidedly a French name."

The woman cast a greatly annoyed look at each of them, and then her sharply expressive eyes said to the girl as plainly as words could have done: "Young lady, hereafter keep your lips closed in affairs not pertaining to yourself."

Turning to the man, she said, "I bought the picture because I got it at the low rate of one hundred dollars, and because I fancied it for its resemblance to a child I once knew, that is all."

"I," he replied, "once had a dear child, singularly like the one portrayed here, in eyes, features, color, expression. It was stolen from me, but I would be almost willing to give my most sacred oath, that if this is not the actual picture it was yet taken from the one which I lost. I wish you would sell it to me."

"Sell it?"

"No, Monsieur, I would part with anything else among my worldly goods rather than with it."

The man looked at her keenly, but avoided an utterance of any thought which might have crossed his mind, suggested by her close attach- ˟ ment to the painting.

He was a close observer and student of the human face, and of its varied shades of character, so that, in the heavy black eyes and sharp features he saw the impression of a spirit that would go a long way in a compromise where money was the balancing power as against the affections; there- fore he was not daunted at what seemed, upon a surface view, to be an absolute refusal on her part.

"I will give you," he said, "five hundred francs for it, which ought to be a fair recompense in con- sideration for what you paid for it."

"Do you think I would part with it for any such price?" she asked scornfully. "I am not the fool to do it, I assure you."

"Double it then, if you will," said the man.

"Not for the double of it, Monsieur."

"Tripple it then."

"Not yet for the triple."

"Quadruple it."

"Not for double, triple, nor quadruple, will I be tempted," she screamed vehemently.

Still she looked at him in a bewildered sort of way, and thought that he must certainly be a very rich man, indeed, to make offers of that sort.

"Come, let us be moving," she said to Agnes, who, after the telling look from her mistress, had commenced to fix up the broken trunk and to re-arrange the things in order.

"You are a simpleton, old woman," said a man in a blouse, who was one among the growing crowd attracted by the loud words of Madame. "I have a cousin, who is an artist, and he can do much finer work than is shown in a daub like that. Ma foi! wouldn't he jump at any such prices as has been offered to you for one of his paintings?"

"Come, woman," said the elderly man, "I will give to you three thousand francs for the picture and not one sou more. Think of it, as compared with the sum which you gave for it, and then give me your decision."

Not yet would her obduracy give way, but she said to him aside, that she would consider his bargain.

He took from his pocket a card, and writing upon it the words, "Henri de Ivry, Boulevardes des Fontaines, Rue a St. Denis," handed it to her.

Then he drew his heavy traveling coat about him, and with a white and jeweled hand gracefully lifted his hat from his brow, as he made a parting bow to herself and Agnes.

The act, small as it was, revealed him in a new light, as the sun is sometimes suddenly seen by the removal of a small cloud from its surface; for instead of the well-to-do tradesman or master mechanic which he had appeared to be, the high intellectual forehead and nameless air of the cultured nobleman was seen.

Madame hailed another conveyance, the first having left them, and soon the now filled trunk, with coils of rope bound about it, and along with themselves, were rolling along the noisy streets.

"He is certainly a gentleman," silently soliloquized the little woman, "and how strange that he should have taken so violent a fancy to my child-picture?"

Then she went off into a dreamy reverie which was unbroken until they reached the cottage.

Here they found everything in readiness for their arrival, the keepers, Jacques and the maid, having been apprised of it by letter.

Madame was quite pleased at the appearance of the premises, as nothing had been neglected.

The horse and phaeton had been kept in good condition, with no appearance of undue usage during her absence; the vegetables from the small garden had been carefully garnered into the cellar for future use, and the St. Catherine pears rested in their golden juice like as many balls of crystal.

Upon an examination of the entire premises from cellar to attic, she declared that she had been a most fortunate woman in her selection of servants. Honest and efficient in a high degree, they had both proved themselves to be.

Not very much thought had she given toward the man who had made the brilliant offer for her treasure.

She hung it upon the wall of the parlor, declaring that he, or any one, must be a madman truly, to think for a moment that she would part with it for any amount of money.

He, it would seem, had made an overestimate of her character, as to its element of avarice. He did not know that a love, which is certainly the strongest of human passions, was controlling her heart in the matter.

He was under the conviction that, by the means stated, she had gotten hold of a copy of his picture, and for that, and for still another reason, perhaps more potent, he was determined to possess it at any price.

That the owner had any personal connection with it, he did not surmise.

Madame was congratulating herself upon spending a most enjoyable winter season, that is if her health, which was now somewhat delicate, should so improve as to admit of it.

She proposed any amount of visits to theatres, concerts and other places of entertainment for herself and Agnes, and, perhaps, she told her, that during the Christmas season they would run down to Ville de Varley to see her cousin, and where she said, jestingly, that Agnes might again see her rustic lover.

There is an adage current among the French people which says, that "No one knows what hangs at the end of his nose," and most surely the little woman with the long appendage of that sort was no exception to the homely aphorism.

She went down town, after the fashion of one of mother Goose's heros, but not exactly with the same intentions.

In this case it was to buy some edibles for Polly, who, like herself, was somewhat indisposed.

While shopping in one of the principle streets she heard the unfortunate news, that the Bank dw Commerce, where all of her money had been deposited, had been so run upon by its patrons on account of an evil report which had got into circulation as to its liabilities, that it had been compelled to close its doors.

She refused to believe the tale at first, thinking it to be but idle gossip, but upon investigation she found it to be correct and, also, that twenty-five per cent. was all that might be expected by the depositors.

Sorrowful enough was such news to her, as it was to all in her situation.

To be sure, she still had the cottage, but what was that as a means of subsistance? "One cannot eat the four walls," she mused, "and how ever will I be able to send Agnes back to her home?"

This question bothered her more than all of the rest.

She felt physically unable to resume, at present, at least, her business as an organizer of theatrical

or operatic entertainments, or to do anything else
whereby a living might be gotten.

As to setting the girl adrift to shift for herself,
in a strange land of whose language she knew
but little, why, certainly, she could not do that.

All these things she thought about as Jacques
drove her home in the phaeton.

Arrived there, her first impulse was to tell
Agnes, but upon further consideration she thought
it best to wait for a few days; and perhaps by that
time she might hear of a better realizement from
her investment, than at first had been anticipated.

Time passed and no better arrangement could
be made, by the bank officials, and she was
compelled to yield to the inevitable.

During the time though, she came to a conclu-
sive resolution in case of the worst. It was to sell
the picture.

Then she told Agnes all about her trouble, and
her determination, saying, that by this means she
might be enabled—through strict economy—to
live and to send her home, when desirable.

She said no more on the subject then, but one
would not need to look close at the pale, pinched
features of her face, and the dark circles about
her eyes, to tell what a secret agony had been
hers to make the sacrifice.

After the sale should be consummated, she
meant to discharge both Jacques and the maid,
and to supply their place by the labor of herself
and Agnes.

Together, then, with the latter and the picture,

she set off in the phaeton, Jacques as driver, to search for the designated residence on the St. Denis road.

They came to it in a short time, as it lay not more than a few miles from the city confines, where no inquiry was necessary, as the ample lawn, with its two superb fountains, casting up their silvery spray under the twin rows of poplars and of beech was a fair indication of the directions given them by the owner.

A porter's lodge stood in one corner of the shaded square, and from it a graveled road led up a distance of two hundred paces or more to where the building stood.

The house was quite modern, certainly not built after the fashion of a castle, and why it should be called one was more than Madame Du Boise could comprehend. She was not aware that its recent erection had been on the site of a very ancient military kind of place, dating back to medieval times, and that custom had caused its name to descend to the new house.

The porter at the lodge was at first somewhat chary as to permitting them an entrance, but, upon a display of his master's card, his objections were withdrawn and they were allowed to proceed upon their way.

The place was a great square, formed of four walls of the reddest of brick, in trimmings of drab, a mansard roof, four great bay windows, two in a tier, on either side of the broad doorway at the head of the marble steps. An open piazza ran the entire length of the building on either side, upon which doors and windows opened.

This was all that it contained in the way of architectural adornment.

Of towers, turrets, oriels and porches it was utterly destitute.

But the grounds about it were magnificent.

The lawn itself, with its boulevarded frame, was an emerald gem in the spring and summer, and even now it looked fine back of the crystal fountains with the brown autumnal leaves blowing over its surface. Past this, to the right of the building, was the flower garden in circles and parteres, and to the left side the greenery and hot beds where blooming exotics and ripening fruit of the tropics were seen.

Back of the house and its contiguous buildings, as far as the vision extended, lay the rich farm lands of the chateau, in gently swelling upland and meadow, in park and in woodland.

The room into which they were ushered by a very polite waiting-man in a livery of red and drab—like the outside of the house—was a small one to the left, opening upon one of the bay windows.

It seemed to be a kind of reception room for temporary callers, and was covered with a fine Persian carpet, with chairs in purple velvet, and portieres at the windows of scarlet damask, wrought in oriental designs with thread of gold.

The walls were of paper in a delicate pink, with clusters of silver frosted leaves, and sprays of ivy.

A superb jardinier of fine workmanship stood in the center of the bay window, with a mass of delicate cream-blossomed vines falling all over it and sending their sweet fragrance throughout the room.

From this apartment another was visible through the half open folding doors, evidently a gentleman's private sitting room, to judge from what was to be seen in the way of cigar holders, gilded cuspidors and lounging seats.

In that room a fire of sea-coal was brightly burning in its burnished grate, and an easy chair drawn near to it was vacant but spoke of a recent occupancy. This was indeed the room where the owner spent the greater part of his time, as it contained his library, and might at any minute be, by the wide doors, thrown into one with the front apartment. He was not there now, but upon the reception of Madame's card he soon made his appearance from a side door.

His suit of black displayed his fine figure to perfection, and his dark hair and mustache was scarce what one might look for in a man of his age, seventy-five being the number of his years.

A pleased expression passed over his fine features as he extended his hand first to Madame Du Boise, and then to Agnes.

"I see," he said complaisently, "that you have taken the trouble to find me. May I hope that you have accepted my proposal as to the sale?" he asked, coming to business at once.

He was nearly certain of as much, as from his
dressing room in an upper story, he had looked
down upon Jacques sitting patiently in the
pheaton, with the object of his wish in a covering of muslin leaning beside him.

"Yes," said Madame Du Boise, "I have met with a
severe loss since I saw you. Very severe indeed
—in a financial way—otherwise I assure you,
Monsieur, that I should never have taken the
trouble to hunt you up."

Then she told him all about the closure of the
bank, a circumstance which he had already heard
through his paper of the consequent disappear-
ance of her small fortune, and her compulsion to
accede to his proposal.

At the conclusion Monsieur rang for a servant
and ordered coffee, cakes fruit, and wine, and
when these were brought for his visitors, he
went out to have the picture removed to the
room.

There seemed to be some talismanic effect about
the work of the humble American artist, who
really knew nothing of her art but that which
nature had taught her; as the dignified aristocrat,
when the casing had been removed, evinced
almost as much emotion at sight of it as the plain
plebian woman had ever done upon a like contemplation.

True, he did not shower kisses of affection upon
it, for men are seldom so demonstrative of their
feelings; but the look of admiration with which
he regarded, mingled, too, with a deeper emotion,

was a sufficient warrant that his heart was stirred in no ordinary way.

When the money came to be paid there was a scene.

Madame refused to touch it.

"I cannot part with the picture," she said, passionately, "it would kill me, it is all I have in the world to love!" and she arose to her feet as if to take it away with her.

"Calm yourself," said De Ivry, sternly, as he gently pushed her back into her seat. "Are you mad? What is it to you, a mere fancied resemblance, as you say, to a child of a friend, that you should so care for its retention?"

"And what is it to you?" she demanded, "that you should so much wish for its possession?"

"It is the likeness of by boyhood's home, as well as that of my ancestors for many generations," he said. "There—pointing to the canvass—is the green lawn upon which I have played, the old trees, the fair flowers and the grand castle, just as I remember them. The old home is no more, it was destroyed during the siege."

"It is not the original, but it is better. It is well executed, I say, and the painter, be she who she may, under a good developing process would be able to work wonders in her line."

"But the boy?" cried the woman, excitedly, "I care nothing for the scenery, tell me only of the boy. Whose child is he?"

"Oh yes, the boy, I was just about to speak of him."

He is also to me much the dearest object of all. He is my own son, or the orginal was, rather, Victor De Ivry."

At the name of Victor the woman started.

The old feeling that had came upon her when first she met this man that, as in a dream she had seen either him or some one like him before, came to her in an intensified form.

A suspicion flashed upon her mind.

Then she made a mental determination to tell him all of the truth concerning her life, let the consequences be what they might.

"And I," she addressed him again, "have a claim of the same sort. The picture is the exact likeness, not of the child of a friend, but that of my own child."

"Your child?" he asked, incredulously, looking at her from head to foot.

"How could a creature of her kind ever be mother to a child like this?" was his mental query.

He did not know of the change that time had wrought in the woman, nor in the years fled that she might have laid claim to some beauty at least, after her grisette style. Neither did he know that little of her blood had been traceable in her son, he was all his father.

"Your child?" he asked sharply, all the suavity of his former manner gone, and in its place the commanding voice of a superior addressing what might have been his meniel, or a beggar, soliciting alms at his hand. All the difference of their

respective positions, socially, was clearly expressed in his way of saying the two words, as only it
can be expressed by those in whose veins flow the
blood of generations who have been accustomed
to hold themselves apart, as of superior clay, to
the mass of their fellow mortals.

Madame Du Boise was no fool and not so easily
intimidated as he probably expected, so she replied
straightforwardly; "yes, my child."

"And who, then, was its father?" he interro-
gated, pointedly.

"His father was, as I claim, my husband,
although he married me under the name of Victor
Du Boise, which I afterwards learned was an
assumed one. His real name I never learned, but
I do know that whoever his family are, they are
of the aristocracy of France."

"He left me just four months from the date of
our marriage, twenty-eight years ago, without
saying a word, except to press a sum of money
into my hand as he was leaving; bidding me at
the time to use it carefully. I afterward received
a letter from him, dated at Lyons, in which he
told me of the fraud which he had practiced upon
me, as to his name, and that the marriage was invalid; and as he was about to leave France I
would see him no more."

"Six months after my babe was born, a beautiful boy, and I called him Victor, after his father,
for, Monsieur, they were as like as pea is to pea or
cherry is to cherry."

"O such a handsome boy, Monsieur! with his

father's noble head and forehead, his joyous blue
eyes and light curling hair!"

"My money lasted me until my child was able
to walk and then it gave out, and I was necessi-
tated to cast about for some sort of work, as a
means of subsistance for myself and boy. I could
have gone back to the factory whence Victor had
taken me, but that would have been the means of
a daily separation from my darling, and I could
not endure the thought of that, so I sewed,
washed, and did anything that was honest, so
that I might keep him by me."

"I never again cared to receive the attention of
any man. In truth I still loved Victor, notwithstanding his cruel treatment, and cherished a hope
that he would some day relent and return to me.
I was sure that he would, had he but a glimpse of
our bonnie boy, for how, I argued, could he resist
loving anything so like himself?"

"Well, the years went by until little Victor was
five years old, then he caught a malignant fever
that was raging in the neighborhood and in three
days I was obliged to lay his idolized form in
the ground."

"He is burried in one of the cemeteries of Paris,
and I struggled hard to have him laid away as
decently as possible."

"After this, I, still a very young woman, attended a night school, where I obtained the rudiments
of the education which I have since built up, and
then for awhile I was on the stage; until I commenced to organize and to drill troupes on my

own account. In this way I have traveled over most of the United States of America; and it was there—as I have before said—that I bought the painting so strangely like my boy, and there I also engaged the services of this young girl."

"Since the days of my desertion I have visited many clairvoyants, fortune-readers and mediums, who tell me that Victor, my husband, as I claim him to be, is dead. I instinctively know that he is."

"Yes, he is dead," mechanically said De Jury, all the tone of hauteur gone out of his voice, and an ashy hue settled upon his face.

"He was my son, and he died in the old castle at Auvignon."

"He came home to me twenty-five years ago from South America, ill and dying, so that in three months time from his arrival I laid his body by the side of his long dead mother in the tomb of our fathers."

"He was the only son that God had given me, and to think that such infamy as this should come to me now! I knew that his life had been broken by what is considered pardonable dissipation in the young, but that he had departed from the morality of his house in this wretched manner, I had no thought!"

"You may be misled as to his identity," suggested Madame Boise.

"No, I am correct," said he. "There is another link in the chain of evidence, indeed, a most powerful one, which I have not yet mentioned."

"I had, besides Victor, an only daughter, Adele. She eloped with a miserable artist, who had been engaged at the castle to retouch some old paintings. His name was Jannaux, and for some reason they carried away with them the picture of the old home and of her brother, as a memento, I suppose, of the place she was so basely to desert. I never afterward heard of them, farther than that they had settled somewhere in America—in Canada, I think—so that I am almost certain that the young artist who painted this one is my granddaughter, named after her grandmother, my dead wife, Eldie."

"You see," he went on, with a sardonic smile, "that the conduct of my two children has proven the fact that good blood and noble surroundings are no barrier against the sins of humanity. They have been no blessing to me. Many a beggar's offspring have been full dutiful to him."

"To be sure, you must be well enough skilled, with your intelligence in the laws of Roman Catholic countries, to know that your marriage with my son, as he himself told, cannot be considered legal, as by the Council of Trent clandestine unions are to be void and invalid."

"I am no Roman Catholic," she replied, rising to her feet again, in her anger, "and I do claim to be the true wife of Victor. I am no wanton, I can tell you, and my child was born without taint. He was all right, I say. I will tell it to the world, my darling little Victor was all right."

As if overcome by her excitement, she sank back to her chair.

The old man took two or three rapid turns about the room and then paused before her.

"Neither am I a Roman Catholic," he said. "The current of the martyrs of Languedoc flows through my heart. I have, however, thrown away much of their extraneous folly. I no longer believe in the barbarous creed of the elect and nonelect by irrevocable doom."

"You say that you are no wanton, and that your child was born all right. In the name of heaven, woman, are you superstitious enough to believe that God ever sends an immortal soul here in any other way, and do you believe that you or it should be called by any name of infamy for any act or circumstance, when thousands of men all over the world are openly transgressing the seventh commandment, and yet go free of everything that might cause social ostracism?

"There is where I take issue with our so-called civilization. Women are considered, theoretically at least, as being the weaker of the two sexes only where passion is concerned, and here, if she fail to be a Judith or a Susannah, she must hear all sounds from Ebal, or the mount of cursing, forever, so far as this life goes.

"Calverism or Roman Catholicism, in the graciousness of Christian charity—what a burlesque on the name!—will allow herself and her innocent child a loophole whereby, with due repentance and a proper humiliation, through their soujourn here, they may, perchance, get into the home of the blessed after death."

Madame Du Boise was surprised, thunderstruck almost, to hear words of this sort coming from the lips of this stately aristocrat, who, despite his ultra views, was politically a legitimist of the most pronounced type. For republicanism—so-called—he had no use.

Gambetta had been to him but a vulgar demagogue, Thiers, Grevy, Carnot, but political upstarts, without the principles of the cause they espoused.

"They have," was his comment, "all the inconsistency of their American brethren, who built up a stupendous slave mart under a government whose shibboleth was human equality!"

The strain upon the nerve system of Madame Boise had been so intense during this interview that she suddenly became quite ill, so ill, indeed, that there was no possibility of her being able to leave the mansion that day.

For this reason Monsieur de Jury dismissed Jacques from the place, bidding him to come out again on the morrow.

Then Madame Boise was assisted by a serving-woman to an appartment up stairs, where every attention was given her.

When the next day arrived she was no better but worse, so that Jacques was the second time sent away without her, and Monsieur de Jury deemed it best to call a physician.

Meantime he ran over to Cambiensis, a village

twenty miles from Paris, and where, through
Agnes, he learned from the sick woman, that she
had been married by a clergyman whose name
she did not know. Agnes went to Paris to see
about the cottage and to make arrangements for
the two servants to stay there until the convales-
cence of their mistress would permit her return.

In a place no larger than Cambriensis, where
changes were few, every clergyman for many
years back had remained in the place, but none of
them remembered having married any one by the
name of Boise, neither was any record of such
marriage to be found in the church books. From
this De Ivry suspicioned that in all likelihood the
entire affair, minister and all, was fictitious, "for,"
he argued, "if my son could perpetrate one-half
of a base deed, why not all?"

His feelings had undergone quite a revolution
in regard to the possession of the picture, since
the recent unfolding of this phase of his son's
character. He was no more. Yet his father's
intense nature could not contemplate a memory
of him without some abatement of affection.
Even parental love is blunted by too rough treatment.

With the thought that perhaps a present of it
might prove a balm of healing to her who seemed
so much to wish for it, he, accompanied by Agnes,
went to her room and made a giving up of
it in her favor, allowing her to retain its price
also.

These were dreary days for the girl.

Madame was imperious in her demand to have her constantly by her side.

The room was pleasant enough, but a continuous waiting upon an invalid is irksome at best, and how much more irksome to her to whom the service had never before fallen?

There came times of release, though, when the sick woman slept, or could, by persuasion, be lenient enough to allow another to take her place. Then she would run down to the greenery, with its vines, its shrubs, its palms and ferns, or the conservatory where everything was a mass of bloom, and where the species of orchid sobrolia and odontoglassa, with their butterfly forms, were so charming.

How she did wish that Robert Orme could share with her in an admiration of their airy grace!

Then, again, she would ramble over the oddly winding paths of the flower garden, with its precise, artificial arrangement, but which, to her, was not half so enchanting as the picturesque old garden at Ville-de-Varley, just as the poet who becomes lost in the lofty abstractions of thought, is not so sweet as he who keeps close to nature's simplicity.

The house was a pleasing study to her. She had never before witnessed anything nearly so grand as the great parlor, with its corbels and casings of wood of Mexico, its velvet-lined walls of gold and crimson, and its mantle of ebony marble. Was ever carpet more brilliant hued, were ever chairs more soft and yielding? And the curtains which draped the windows. There was surely a fortune in the fine Mechlin lace and the heavy embroidery which composed them she was sure.

Then there was the picture gallery, with many a fine old painting in all the rich coloring of a Rubens or a Titian, the grace of a Raphael and the mingling lights and shades of a Rembrandt, together with portraits of the De Ivrys' of many generations.

The armory, too, was to be seen, with its collection of blunderbusses, spears, lances, swords, and armor of ring and of plate, with plumeless helmets and broken shields.

The family coats of arms, with their varied devices, was also here, in eagles, falcons, flowers, fruits, and grains, and one—a silver lion, rampant on a field of blue—had the faded and blurred motto, "*Qui voulait excelle*," which, by the aid of her book of French, she was able to translate, "Who, wishes excels;" and the pictorial ensign meant that one must have the wish with all the force of a roused lion, in order to obtain the desired excellence.

Sometimes Monsieur De Ivry was kind enough to take her for a drive in his fine carriage all about the plantation, or through the dripping park, where bird music was no longer heard, only the sigh of the breeze or the rush of the heavy wind as they swept along the leafless branches; and under foot no living thing to be seen but patches of green moss or of whitened lichen among the wreaths of dead leaves; or they would take the broad, smooth road toward St. Denis, so famed for its flowers, its fountains, and its beautiful homesites.

The old gentleman was very kind to her.

He had noticed her assiduous and uncomplaining attentions toward Madame Boise, and to him this alone was a source of admiration. She was a good girl, he was sure, and, besides, the sick woman herself had spoken warmly in her praise, as to her self-sacrificing devotion for her parents.

But all of his kindness, all of the fair Gallic scenes, and her grand surrounding could not, at times, prevent a feeling of weary unrest from coming upon her as she thought of her humble friends across seas; and of all the dear ones there; ending always in a violent spell of home-sickness, and a wish that she might be able to see Madame Boise well enough to dispense with her services and to allow of her departure to America.

CHAPTER VIII.

"A pretty fellow you are! Do you know that you have cheated me out of eighty acres of good land? Of course you know it, there is no need to ask the question. You knew that you were swindling me and others, at the time you made your fair statements; but I'll be even with you yet, mark my word."

The speaker, pale with anger, shook his fist toward a figure with a face almost as pale as his own, as it cowered close to the lobby wall, leading to one of the most prominent business blocks in the city.

He was but one of the crowd of beligerents, all equally as full of wrath as was himself.

He ceased for a moment or two as if to regain breath, and to collect a supply of denunciating epithets before resuming the thread of vituperation, but ere he had time to commence anew another took it up for him.

"I am also one out of whom you have taken a blood-sucker's bite by your false deal. Where is the lot, for which I paid to you three hundred dollars, with the assurance that in a very short time I might be able, by sale or trade, to double my money? Where is it I say? In the land of no where or nearly as bad. Miles away from here in a swamp that is covered by water in summer, and by a muskrat town on ice in the winter. O, but your a sweet one, ar'nt you? Give me back my money, damn you, or else come out here and we shall see which is the better man of the two. I'll take it out of your miserable carcass!"

This speaker was too plethoric a build to be pale, he was purple and bloated with anger. He made a lurch toward the guilty wretch who evidently did not care to measure the strength of his muscle against an opponent of this sort. He clung still closer to the wall and his foe was kept off by the threat of some uninterested bystanders, who spoke of calling for police interferance if the peace was broken in this way.

"He's a sneak and a villain," said another voice.

"I should like to see him whipped soundly. I traded off two lots in a desirable location for his worthless stuff. They belenged to my wife, and I induced her to part with them, so that my family peace is broken. I shall never hear the last of the fine bargain which I have made!"

"I have mortgaged my home," said a fourth, "in order to raise money to pay for the fraud. Of course it will be sacrificed, as the tarnal lots cannot be sold for enough to pay the rate for a good soul's passage through purgatory."   .

This raised a laugh among the unbitten.

"What's all the fuss about!" asked a tall, clerical looking man, who had just joined the group.

"What's it about," shouted the plethoric individual, his anger not one whit abated. "I can tell you what it's about. That scoundrel yonder was possessor to a tract of land which he defined as being most excellent for building purposes, and said it was near a lake north of the city limits. Well, he made out, gentlemen, to sell a good portion of it at prices suitable to land of the described location, but when the buyers came to look up their purchase, they found it in section thirty-five, township thirty-four, range west, just forty miles from the city, lying north truly, and near a lake of the same name, and this comes of having more than one natural feature of a State to bear the identical handle. They seemed fixed on purpose for the benefit of such sharks as he. It proved to be swamp land, and barren, sandy bluffs, unfit for anything, unless it might be to put this villian out to browse upon for a term of years like Nebuchadnezzer of old. I should, in that case, have no mercy upon him!"

"Nor I! nor I! nor I!" shouted several voices in succession.

"Why, he's ruined me," said the man with the mortgaged home. "He's got the money for which myself and family shall be turned into the street. But I must and will have my money back! I cannot stand his fraud, it is too bad!"

"Well," said a bystander, "why don't you all band together and pursue the same plan that he has; or, in other words, proceed to sell your lots according as they were sold to you, as the suburbs; city suburbs, you know, may be made to extend a long way."

"O, yes! that would be fine indeed," answered one of the gulls. "To make ourselves as mean as he, and by so doing become fit subjects for the penitentiary. I think there are none here who would be ready for an act of that sort."

"Perhaps," said the clerical looking man, "that if you all weigh well your motives in the transaction, it will be found that you were not altogether guiltless. He, it seems, a skillful fisherman, held out a gilded bait, and had no trouble in finding fish enough to bite without question, as to the rightousness of the thing."

"Did it never strike you, gentlemen, that the land was too cheap, at your buying price, for the supposed location? Nor that the persons to whom you should sell, that is, if you doubled your money, would have to pay to you a sum altogether too much, on your speculation? No, you never thought of that."

"So long as we are not to be bled, so long as there was something to be made in any way easier than the strictly honorable one imposed upon our first parents, when they left Eden, you were satisfied!"

"You were willing to make any sacrifice in order to gain something for nothing."

"But in all such movements, recollect, that some one has got to pay for this easy filling of your purse. In the case of a land boom, so called, it is extremely hard when it falls upon the the mechanic or laborer, who by this fictitious value, is either deprived of the benefits of a roof he may call his own, or else is driven far out from the center of his work, so that to make for himself and family a living is impossible."

The man was a reformer, a single, or land tax theorist, and at his words, the culprit who, until now, had heard all of the abuse heaped upon him, with a silent tongue, took courage to speak, and his invectives were fully as strong as any that had been hurled at him.

"You'r all a lying, sneaking set of numskulls, you are indeed!"

"If you find that you are cheated whose fault is it? Why did you not investigate the matter? You had your own eyes; you had your own ears; and your own mouths to inquire, and the stuff that you have trucked off for my bargain is scarcely worth anything."

"I, though, am willing to give up some of the money, at least, to those very much wronged individuals, who, it would seem, know more of billingsgate than they do of business principles, any way the hen-pecked husband, and the one who was silly enough to risk the home of his family for the sake of a larger piece of fortune's cake, if they will call at my office at ten o'clock, sharp, to-morrow morning."

Then the fraudulent dealer in real estate, forgetting the imputation which he had just cast at his opponents, as a protection against their just charges, which would have put to shame the famous war words between Daniel O'Connor and the huckster woman of Dublin; after which he managed to slip away unnoticed by the crowd.

A tall, mild looking man also left about the same time, and took his way to his suburban home.

It was William Clipper, and he was one of the dupes of the sharp trader.

His little all, the savings of several years, had been invested in one lot, with the hope that a miraculous advance and rapid sale would enable him, in a short time, to bring to Hannah a marriage dowry, which would so surprise and please her that all objections to their union—on that score—might be removed.

He, who was so opposed to the accumulation of wealth in an unjust manner, had never considered it a wrong for the holder of land to take advantage of a rise in the market, so long as he kept to strict business principles. Therefore he had entered upon the small speculation without the least straining of his conscience.

He had small faith that the dealer would keep his word, as to a restitution, even to the persons mentioned; much less to himself, in case he made application, and as to entering a suit in law against him, that seemed infeasable, as a case could not, in his judgment, be well substantiated.

The barren truth—which is not always as fair as poets and philosophers make it to appear—stared him in the face. He had been badly fleeced, like a confiding lamb who is caught in the toils of the wolf, and that ended it.

What would Jaax, his neighbor, say when he heard about it? he asked himself.

He most likely would hear of it, for, though not a reading man himself, yet some of his more literary neighbors would tell him from those worse than gossips, the daily papers.

Then he gave a few bitter thoughts toward those recepticles of petrified wisdom; mentally deciding that, though the freedom of the press was a good thing, yet a slight repression of its prerogative would be beneficial to society, at any rate to himself just at present.

There was Hannah, too, to think about.

She, also, would certainly in time become an apprisant of the bungling piece of work in all its stupidity. Hannah! for whose sake it had been done!

She, he was sure, would now think less of his business capabilities than ever.

Was ever lover more unfortunate since the days of fairy lore?

Was ever woman so hard to be won since the time of knighthood?

He loved her as much as ever, and for the sake of securing a more elevated value in her estimation, had tried various monied schemes.

Firstly, he essayed to become a civilized cowboy, if such a being can exist, and, with this view, went to the depth of twenty dollars in his purse, spending it on as many young calves, but luck was against him. Some of them died while still too young to care for themselves, and those which had hardihood enough to reach a state of mature calfhood, were stolen one night by cattle thieves.

Then he went into the chicken business, but the cholera broke out among them, so that in a short time his well-arranged coops, with their glass windows facing the southern warmth, and their fortified backs fighting the northern winds, were destitute of inhabitants. Every feathered and blooded creature was dead, despite this liming, scouring, and vigorous use of cayenne pepper!

He began to fear that Poctolus would never smile upon him!

One morning about a week after the discovery his failure as a skillful speculator, he was walking through the woods back of his habitation with some sticks for a drop-trap under one arm and a short-handed garden hoe in the other.

He was too much taken up with his gloomy cogitations, to notice, what upon another occasion would have been a scene of enthusiastic delight, that the trees were covered with a mantle of white, soft as ermine or eider, made brilliant by the early sun's rays in a million of sparkling gems.

The law of silence which in winter holds in imperial repression all sounds, save when it is broken by the sweeping tempest, as it comes to trample upon it in its power, was over all with its mystic influence, only his own footsteps making the least encroachment as they crushed the pliant carpet under them.

No sign of life was seen, save a solitary squirrel, as it scudded over the snow with nimble feet and timid eyes toward its burrow in some aged oak.

Clipper was thinking, and among other thoughts, of course, Hannah had her full share.

The old adage runs, "Think of Satan and he will appear."

Now, no one among all the spinster's acquaintances thought quite badly enough of her—Mrs. Desmond included—to put her upon an equal footing with this baleful personage, but for this one time she appeared to fit into the proverb exactly, as, upon raising his organs of vision from the ground at a slight noise he looked squarely upon her trim, wiry form, with its brown dress and dark cloak.

On one of her arms rested the handle of a small basket, and within the circle of the other a paper parcel.

Clipper was upon the ignoble errand of endeavoring to snare to its death a creature whose only fault lay in the fact that it was more weak than himself, but Hannah was bent upon either saving life or else to alleviate its suffering, for she was on her way to Eldie Jannaux with dainties for eating and herbs for medicine.

Not expecting to meet her at this time in the morning, it being quite early, her appearance caused him to bring himself to a sudden and rather surprised stop.

"Why, Hannah," he said, as he shifted the hoe and extended to her his hand, "You must be an early riser to be out so soon in the morning."

She took his hand mechanically, while a hardness more than usual came into her dark eyes.

Her lover noticed the expression and groaned inwardly, as he considered that its advent boded no good toward him.

"Yes, I am an early riser. People who have to earn their living by labor must not dilly-dally morning, day, nor evening. Time means money to them and money means time."

Hannah was not of the sort who are able to put their thoughts into long or uncommon words, but she could express herself with sufficient force and clearness to be well understood, especially in the line of fault-finding.

"High-sounding words," she used to say, "are just used by some folks to show how much more they know than other folks."

No pedant was she, so far as books are concerned, but when it came to housekeeping—; *then* she was the greatest pedant alive! for there is just where you will find as much of the "show-off" as anywhere in life, not in all cases though, for earnest workers are there who make no comment upon themselves or others, just as the same sort are found among lettered people.

Her brief homily upon the question of time and money was divined, as to its meaning, by him. The storm was brewing, and soon it fell about his defenseless head!

He, for the first time, noticed the chaste beauty about them as his eyes wandered restlessly away from her face to the jeweled vista before him; and he quickly took advantage of it to break the ominous spell, and to divert his companion's attention from the theme which he knew was engaging her thoughts at the moment.

What a charming sight we have in the snow-clad ground and trees, with their myriads of sparkling gems, and, as I live, if there isn't a bluejay; the first I have noticed this winter, though some seasons they are plenty enough.

The bird at that moment perked its beautifully tufted head, extended its blue-and-black barred wings, and noiselessly sailed away to the top of a distant cottonwood.

Their eyes followed it almost involuntarily.

"Yes, the woods look well enough, but as to birds I never did care much for them, they are such mischievous creatures. My raspberries are destroyed every year, more or less, by them. Speaking about them, though, brings the old saying to mind that 'a bird in the hand is worth two in the bush.'"

Her bright, piercing eyes looked straight into his milder ones, which caused him to wince perceptably, still he went on with his evasive talk.

"It is some time since I have had any birds worth mentioning. I went out along with Robert Orme last fall after chickens and partridges, but got only a brace of the latter for our pains."

"I should think," said Hannah, "that you would find something more honorable to do than to be idling about that way."

Her lover colored, as he asked testily, and with more spirit than she thought him capable of showing, "Did you ever know of my doing anything dishonorable, Hannah?"

"Well, no; not exactly; but I'm sure that trying to get something without fairly and squarely working for it is not very honest, in my way of thinking."

"And when did I do that?" he asked. "You seem to know more of my business than I do myself."

"Well, I only know what the whole neighborhood knows about your foolishly throwing away your three hundred dollars upon a catch-penny scheme."

"Oh! but you are smart! A man of your age, too! I was surprised to know that you had so much money about you, and truly I must allow you some credit for your saving habits—; but—having so much—why didn't you stick to it?"

"It just serves you right, though," went on the spinster. "Why can't people be satisfied without entering into some idle freak of speculation?"

"No good comes of it I am sure."

"O yes, there does, sometimes, Hannah."

"Lots of persons make their fortunes in just such a way."

"Yes, but they are different kind of persons from you. They have some business about them, and don't pay out their money on a blind."

"Well, my money is gone, and its loss seems to be irretrievable. I suppose I am some to blame; but, to put the subject pointedly, how would it have been in your estimation had I been successful in the deal? That is to say, if I had been able to double my means by it?"

"I know," she replied, "that success, like charity, covers a heap of wrong. Success with you would surely have made you stand better among our neighbors."

"It would look as if there were something more than mere shiftlessness about you. Either that, or the keeping of your money, would have suited me better than the stupid work you have done."

Her voice had a broken querulousness in it, that he had never noticed before, and her eyes wore a strongly moistened look.

"I had about half made up my mind——."

She stopped with her sentence unfinished.

"Made up your mind to marry me, Hannah? is that it?"

That is just what she was about to say, but the old spirit of contrariness seized her at that instant, and she said; "no, not that, but that I had a notion to take no notice at all of you this morning, especially as my time is precious. Eldie Jannaux is racked with a cough, she is in need of these things, so good bye Mr. Clipper," and she was gone without further formality; down the snowy way leading to the lake.

Clipper looked after her as he made the silent comment, "well, Hannah I begin to see through you, although you think yourself impenatrable, I believe, with a small show of property, or money on my side, to silence the tongue of gossip more than any other consideration, you would become mine. No doubt her heart has belonged to me all of the time, only she has been too stubborn to admit of it."

"None of the silly, gushing sort is Hannah, none of the women who carry their heart on the outside or their bosom."

With a satisfied smile on his pale features, the fisherman and hunter went on his way, over the glistening ground to where the trees grew thicker and the snow lay in drifted piles; some large, some small, just as the wind had laid them, according to some geometrical law of nature.

He laid his material upon the ground, and then kneeling down, commenced to scrape with his hoe, the upper layer of recently fallen feathery flakes from off the under layer, which had been congealed into a form almost as solid as clear ice.

After a short time of hard labor he had cleared a space large enough for his purpose, and then he arose and brought a log from its leaning posture against a neighboring tree, where it had been deposited by himself, while out wood chopping, the day before.

This he fixed as a dead fall, by driving some sharp sticks into the frozen soil, by means of a hatchet which he drew from a great side pocket in his overcoat.

At the moment of completion of this instrument of death—just as he was about to arise from his stooping posture—his eyes fell upon something glittering among the hard substance at the off side of the trap, much too large it looked for one of the fairy snow-diamonds, and besides it had a more auriferious and substantial face than any of those frail shinners.

His first thought was, "I have scraped out from its hiding place a nugget of the precious mineral."

"Who knows, perhaps the fickle goddess of fortune is about to smile upon me."

Then his judgment told him that these tame bluffs would scarcely be the place for the yellow mineral to crop out, or if, against all likelihood, it did exist here, it must have before this found a discoverer.

To carefully remove the tenacious casing of ice from about it was the work of no great length of time, so that soon it rested in the palm of his hand, not a nugget, but an old-fashioned and beautifully chased locket, such as was much in use a few decades ago, as an ornament for watch chain or necklace.

For every Madame Bluebeard a male mate may be found.

The nymph, Curiosity, does not rule the female gender exclusively.

She sometimes, nay, very often, manages to get her sceptre in full waving sway over the head of some wight of the genus homo.

She so managed upon this occasion, for no sooner had the staid, thoughtful bachelor taken a full view of the superficial beauties of the thing which he held than a strong desire seized upon him to know of its contents.

A few minutes of rubbing and warming between

his two palms made the spring by which it was fastened, pliable enough to open, so that soon his wish was gratified.

As he had suspected, it contained a portrait, not of old style, like its receptacle, but modern, with the impress of that best of all means for obtaining epochs of time; the dress of the individual, coat, shirt-front and tie, all indicative of a lapse of not more than two years since the artist had caught the shadow of the real and brought it to a fixity, an image of its type as the face of the human is the image of its creator.

The countenance was dark, with heavy, clear-cut features, a beetling forehead, fronted by black brows; side-whiskers, resting over wide jaws, and a chin, square with an iron firmness impressed upon it. A singular face, with the unmistakable look of a man of forcible character, strong for either good or evil, according to the path in which his destiny should lead him.

It had led him into the way of evil, as the sequel will show.

CHAPTER IX.

Carnations and smilax! How beautiful are they when skillfully interwoven! Henrietta Dudley was an adept in the art of boquet-making, and this morning in her aunt's parlor she stood, working at one for a throat knot to adorn her own fair self.

Delightfully happy she looked, with a light in her eyes, and a pride on her forehead, for she had recently entered upon a new role; one not often assumed by women of her class, that of a person of business; and what was still more, she had come off victor in the contest, if great financial success may be used as an equivalent for the word, as she had been fortunate in the highest degree.

It came about in this way:

Having heard of a boom in real estate in a town of a neighboring State, she had borrowed from her lover, Charles Lennox, the sum of five hundred dollars.

The loan was given, not without considerable hesitation, as he considered the step one beyond the prerogatives of her sex, and this was distasteful to him in any woman, how much more then in the one to whom he had given his love?

But the affection of his heart overbalanced his

natural antipathy to the proposed course, and then, modern custom argued in her favor.

This, it told him is an age of reform and progression. Old theories and practices were rapidly dissolving under the advancing light of liberal education, and of thought. Women were no longer looked upon as creatures of mere dependence. The simile of the oak and the vine had lost its force. During his own, not very long life, he had noticed cases where the order was entirely reversed, and in most of connubial ties there seemed to be an even balance, a state which precluded either party from the condition of parasiteism.

Looking at the affair in the coloring of these silent reflections, he made up his mind to yield to her request.

Mrs. Desmond was horrified, to use her own expression of feeling.

"She is going beside herself," was her comment.

"To think of a female Dudley undertaking so bold and masculine a step—all, too, for the vulgar thing of feathering her own nest! She is the first one of her race to enter the list of strong minded women and I hope she will be the last."

Hetty took her departure to the place of the flesh-pots where the buzzards were gathering in unprecedented numbers, and a most voracious, gormandizing bird was she among the rest of them.

Either she was possessed of extraordinary foresight and business capacity, or else she met with the particular favor of experienced male advisors, which a very handsome, well-dressed and tolerably intelligent woman would be apt to secure for herself.

She went away with her humble five hundred dollars and returned worth twenty thousand, in a short time! All by the successful manipulation of real estate in the town of a phenominal land-rise.

As she stood upon this bright February morning among the pots of roses, geraniums and other floral beauties, well, then, might she seem as blooming as any of them.

There was also another reason for her bright gladness, and of this last she was thinking most as she gently pulled, twisted and arranged the charming bits of coloring, scarlet and cream, between her shell-tipped taper fingers.

The morning sun just far enough upon his western journey to meet squarely the south looking window, threw his gold transmuting shafts athwart the dark of her hair, lighting it into a thousand gilded threads, and giving to her face a look of brilliancy entrancing in its effects. How grandly beautiful she seemed with her eyes downcast upon her work, the long lashes sweeping her cheek with their gentle curve.

Surely Ariadne was not more peerless among the Goddesses, when she stood before her kneeling Thesius, than was this woman among the daughters of Eve.

So she appeared when the announcement that her lover was at the door surprised her.

It was rather an inopportune time for him to pay her a visit, and she expressed some wonder at it by the least perceptible change of countenance. But that was all.

There was none of the heart-flutterings, none of the exqusite thrillings of pleasure trembling along the nerves, tuning them to that music of love for the one among all others where perfect affinity meets.

The lute within her bosom kept time to the touch of a different hand.

The same statuesque repose, the same self-satisfied look and absorption to the order of the flower-jewel that signalized her before his advent, was upon her.

His early call came about through the mediumship of Clipper.

When that worthy man reached his home after the finding, he took a more scrutinizing look at the locket, and found—what had before escaped his notice—the name "Henrietta" finely lettered in the concave of the covering.

Then his memory reverted to the picnic of a. good deal more than a year ago. To be sure, he reasoned, this trinket belongs to Miss Dudley and she must have lost it at that time, that cruel time when Hannah, he had afterwards heard, tabooed his presence upon pain of her own nonappearance.

Then he planned to carry it to its owner himself that very day, but unforseen circumstances arose to prevent, so that he handed it to Lennox,

whom he met late that night on his way home
from the city.

Clipper opened it at presentation, in order to
show to him the name, as a proof that it belonged
to his betrothed wife. Then Lennox saw the portrait. It was, without doubt, that of the hunter,
who had crossed the path of Hetty and himself,
with the gleam of recognition in his eyes, at the
time of the fall picnic, and of the stranger who
seemed so bent upon watching their movements
at the ball of the previous winter.

Here, then, was a mystery.

He had not, on account of a two days' absence
to a neighboring town, been able to see Hetty since
her return from her business trip, so he intended
to go over to the Desmond cottage that evening,
but the circumstance of meeting with Clipper
hastened his visit.

He had all of the haste of an ardent lover who
wishes an affair, touching upon his jealousy, either
fancied or real, cleared up as quickly as possible.

Hetty advanced into the center of the room as
he came in, and with an air of listless sang froid
took his proffered hand.

A less penetrating man than Lennox could not
have failed to notice her coolness of reception and
her utter want of interest in the man to whom she
had pledged herself in promised wifehood.

He, of course, noticed it, and the fact added
much to his preconceived notion of inconstancy
on her part.

His mind was in too perturbed a state to think

of inquiring as to her success, whether it was good or ill. Indeed, as his love for her had not been in the least tinged by a mercenary coloring, he had, from the first, cared but little for the affair. He had allowed her the necessary money, more out of a fond yielding to her wish than from any other consideration. So much power had this fascinating woman wielded over the strong man.

A few commonplace remarks as to her journey and the subject was dismissed for one of more import, or the one relating to the portrait and its original.

"I have here," he began, "a locket which was found in the woods where we picniced sixteen months ago. It was discovered under the snow by William Clipper, who brought it to me, and, as your name is engraved within, I presume it is yours."

Her color and voice changed somewhat as she answered, "Yes, the locket is mine, as also is the original of the picture." This she said, as she extended her hand and took it from his open palm.

Then she opened it and gazed earnestly at the dark face within.

"Yours?" asked Lennox in a tone of bewilderment. "How am I to understand you, Hetty? Do you mean to say that the man there imaged is anything to you; that he is a relative by blood?"

"None of blood, whatever, she replied calmly. He is my husband, and, as such, mine entirely, and more than a mere blood relative."

"Your husband!" exclaimed Lennox, as he arose

from his seat, pale and agitated, with anger, surprise and mortification, are you, then, a married woman?"

As an answer she drew from her pocket an embossed paper envelope and handed it to him. James Harris and Henrietta Dudley was written upon the back, and upon the sheet within, first the Episcopal benediction, "In the name of the Father, and of the Son, and of the Holy Ghost," followed by a certification that there had been joined in bonds of holy matrimony, by an authorized minister, and in the presence of witnesses, at a town in the State of Illinois, the two persons whose names appeared upon the outside of this certificate, in September of 1884.

Mechanically he handed it back to her.

"I ask from you a clearer testimony than this," he said.

"This, to be sure, tells me that you have been married to this man, but it does not tell me why you should have engaged yourself to me; why you should, in seeming at least, have given me your love. Are you a widow, or a divorced wife?"

He awaited her response with breathless anxiety.

The dying catch at anything, and he was morally dying.

He would have forgiven her all, could she have answered either question in the affirmative, anything so that she might be his.

"Neither," she said, looking at him steadily with her blue eyes.

"He is not dead, nor is he divorced from me, but on the contrary, he is alive and well. We shall, should nothing intervene to prevent, be together in a couple of weeks. If you remember aright, I engaged myself to you under conditions. If nothing happens, if the fates are willing, I think, were my words. I declare to you that I should have kept my vow had these conditions been fulfilled; or, to make things more explicit, in case that my then incarcerated husband should die in the penal institution of his native state before the expiration of his sentence; a thing which, at that time, seemed quite probable."

He was about to speak, but she silenced him by a gesture, and a continuance of her discourse.

"You, no doubt, suppose the person here portrayed, to be identical with the rather mysterious acting man whom we met twice; once, you will recollect, in the garb of a hunter, and again in the lobby of the ball room in the city."

"It is not him, however, but of his twin brother. They are as like as two peas."

"James and I were married clandestinely while I was on a visit to a friend of mine in the State of Illinois. In fact we had never met until we saw one another there."

"One month after marriage, before I had returned to my parents, he was arrested for forgery, tried, convicted and sentenced to the penetentiary for several years. Soon after his imprisonment, his health failed, and death almost stared him in the face for a long while."

"Then I came out here, to find, to my surprise, that his brother was ahead of me, and already fixed in a business way, and also to find, that so soon as my arrival was known to him he was acting the part of a spy upon my conduct."

"I held an interview with him through correspondence, explaining my actions, and this explanation seems to have satisfied him; as I have neither seen nor heard from him until the day of my recent return, when I received a notification from him by mail telling of his brother's release and perfect restoration to health."

"This was a great, I can truly say a joyful surprise to me, as his time had been shortened by one year; the remission made on account of good behavior on his part."

"You see, the fates have been opposed to a marriage with you."

At this Lennox arose, unable any longer to quell his feelings, and facing her he said, "I only wish to ask you one question, Hetty. Do you love this man whom you call by the honored name of husband; this man who has branded his name, and the one you must bear, by a villianous deed?"

"Hush!" she exclaimed excitedly, "I will not hear him maligned! he is mine, recollect. Love him! do you ask? As well as my own life! well enough to die for him if needful."

"Enough," he said as he steadied himself by a hold on the back of the chair from which he had arisen, "I am not the man to upbraid you for your deceitful and utterly heartless bearing toward me.

I only leave you to that which the undeviating
law of recompense will bring to you; that Nemesis
of human actions, who, though long he may be in
paying like for like, yet surely will come. He
never forgets, and sometimes pays with compound interest."

"I need not to ask of you to remember the
episode which came in the last eighteen months
in your life and mine. No danger is there that
you will ever be able to forget it, though much
you should endeavor to erase it from the page of
your memory. The path of evil doings is not so
easily wiped out. To me it has been the sweetest
period that ever came into my existence, and the
sweetest that will ever come into it again, for I
loved you, Hetty, with a strength not often equal-
ed, believing you to be that which you appeared,
an embodiment of what is said by moralists to be
a rare combination—great physical beauty, with
the still greater gift of truthfulness and honor."

"I have been most grievously deceived, and must
needs submit to my own want of perception, and
the consequences of entire disobedience to my
mother's warning voice, for she has always
doubted your sincerity."

In a stupid sort of way, then, as if unable to
properly think what he was about, he took two
rolls of bills—one comprising a loan of five hundred dollars, the other an additional five hundred
as a compensation for its use—from her without
even so much as touching her hand, as a token of
farewell; left the room and the house, stuffing the

parcels into his pocket in so careless a manner that he dropped one before he had gone along the lake road, leading to his home, more than fifty yards.

With a faith rivaling that of the children of Heber in the Shekinah within the Holy of Holies, he had never once suspected her integrity, notwithstanding his mother's vague dislike of her, until it was thus brought to his very face.

The revelation was too sudden not to affect him deeply, almost distractedly, for his nature was not sufficiently volatile enough to throw off a great grief by an outburst of temper. He was not the thundering, terrific avalanche which breaks and spends itself by the force of its own fury and then is as calm in its broken fragments as it was before it took its wild flight; he was rather the smouldering fire which never bursts, or the rumbling ocean which, keeping within its bounds, the elements of turbulence.

Clipper deserved to be known by the cognomen of "find-all," for of all the folks in the vicinity he was the most apt to stumble upon a lost article, be it small or great, valuable or otherwise. This peculiarity arose from a habit, common with him, of always looking upon the ground as he walked.

He was an exact exemplification of the saying of the full ear of wheat being apt to bend downward, in contradistinction to the empty one which invariably assumes an upright posture.

It is to be supposed that in his mind his opponent, Jaax, filled the latter part of the axiom, as

his head was generally erect in the effort to find
out all he could about the business of others.

Clipper, to be sure, was the one who stumbled
upon the roll of bills, lost by Lennox, who had
gone directly home, and under the pretext of in-
disposition, kept his room all day. The next
morning, however, he arose and appeared at table
as calm as usual, with nothing but a slight pallor
and an undefined look of hardness about his face
and eyes, to tell that anything unusual had occurred to upset his equanimity.

After a few days he made up his mind to go to
Montana, where he would make another effort at
success in his profession.

He mentioned nothing whatever of his disap-
pointment. He did not even speak Hetty's name
to his mother, but she, with the instinct of a loving parent, saw that something was wrong with
him, and shrewdly guessed at the cause.

It was what she had all along expected to be
the outcome of his courtship with Miss Dudley.

He never again saw the face of the unprincipled
woman, and the next day he started for the city to
make arrangements for his departure toward the
West.

He met Clipper on the road not far from his
shanty.

He, too, was about to go to the city, where he
meant to make known through the daily papers
the finding of the roll of bills.

He told Lennox about it, but was answered in a
way so abrupt and coarsely startling that it almost

raised the meek man from his feet in a bewildered surprise.

"Curse you, Clipper, are you my evil genius? Why are you always finding something that will serve either as a link in my unhappy destiny or a reminder of it?"

"The money? Do you wish to know whose it is? It is mine, or it was, but I have no use for it. Keep it yourself, man. It would burn my fingers were I to touch it. You may as well know that it is all over between Miss Dudley and me, and this is the interest, at one hundred per cent., of a sum I loaned to her to go upon that speculating tour. I kept my own, and that is all that I want."

"She made a good thing of it, I understand," said Clipper. "Fifty thousand dollars, I believe——"

Lennox stopped him with a sign of impatience.

"Take it, I say, and try to make good use of it. It may be the means of settling you fairly with Miss Shaw."

The modest fisherman blushed like a woman.

That he was pleased beyond expression it is needless to say; so that with many thanks and good wishes for the welfare of the donor, he returned to his humble home, a dozen projects already forming themselves in his mind for its disposal.

CHAPTER X.

"It fell upon ae day, ae bonnie summer's day,
When the clans were 'a' wi Charlie,
That there fell out a great dispute,
Between Argyle an Airlie.

Argyle hae raised a hunder o' his men,
For to come i' the mornin' airly,
And there awa doon, at the back o' Dunkeld,
For to plunder the bonnie house o' Airlie.

Lady Oglebie stans on her high casle wa,
An O, but her heart beats sairly,
For to see Argyle an all o' his men,
Come to plunder her bonnie hame o' Airlie.

Come doon, come doon, Lady Oglebie, he cried,
Come doon till me sae fairly,
Or e'er the morning's clear daylicht,
I'll nae leave a standin' stoon in Airlie.

I wed na come doon prood Argyle, she cried,
Nor come to thee sae fairly,
Not even though by the mornin's licht,
Ye na leave a standin stoon in Airlie.

Argyle in a rage attack't the bonnie Ha,
An his men to the plunderin o' Airlie,
An tears though he saw like the dew-drops fa,
I a low he set the bonnie house o' Airlie.

What is you low cried the brave Lochiel,
That rises this mornin sae Airlie,
By the God o' my kin, cried the young Oglebie,
It's my ain bonnie hame o' Airlie.

It's nae any bonnie hame, nor the lands that I hae,
That grieves me heart sae sairly,
But it is my winsome dame, an the sweet bairns I lett,
They'll be smoored i' the dark rook o' Airlie.

Draw ye'r dirks, draw ye're dirks, said the brave Lochiel,
Unsheathe ye're swords cried Charlie,
An we'll kinle sic a low roon the fause Argyle,
An we'll licht wi a spark oot o' Airlie."

"You're song is too loud, Jessie."

It was the voice of Mrs. Desmond, as she entered the cottage kitchen.

"It's a nice song, and no doubt all of it true, but
don't you know, Jessie, that Mr. Desmond has
been quite ill all night, but now is in a light sleep,
so that I wish the house to be kept as quietly as
possible."

Then she left the kitchen, and went up stairs to
Hetty's room, where that young lady was preparing her trunks in order for an early departure
from the land which had proven so much of a
bonanza to her, for the one that contained her
heart's love; for this unprincipled woman was
altogether capable of a grand passion, only her
object must fill her mental conception of manhood, a thing that Charles Lennox had never done,
could never do, even though she were free to him.
He was of too fine a type for her assimilation.

"Are you going to leave us so soon?" asked her
aunt.

"I think it is time," said Hetty.

"You know that I have delayed my season
for going home by many months."

"Yes, and I suppose that your parents have long
wished to see you, so that upon this consideration
I cannot urge upon you to remain with us longer,
much as we shall all miss you."

"Your uncle is, I am sorry to say, quite unwell
at present. John, too, is somewhat under the
weather, and no wonder, for the dear boy has had
enough to try him of late. It is for his sake that

I came up this morning, to thank you for your
kindness to him, and through him, to us all. It
will, I hope, be sufficient to save to us our home,
which is something."

"A great deal," said her niece, and I am pleased
to be able to give to him the necessary assistance.
I wish that I might do more for him, but you
know, that I had, of course, to pay Charles Lennox
his own out of my money, and out of consideration of his kindness to me, I doubled the amount,
so allowing to him an interest of one hundred per
cent."

Her aunt looked at her in surprise, as she said:

"No, I did not know that. I thought that as
you did not see fit to marry while here, he would
follow you home for that purpose, so that it would
make no difference as to who had the money."

"But I suppose that you have your own ideas,
or business principles, which it is not for me to
gainsay, I, who have never earned one cent that
I might directly call my own."

Hetty's fortunate venture had quite modified
her aunt's ideas about a woman's sphere. It
is in this, as in all else in life. Let a woman
but be able to command a share of the yellow
leaven which keeps life in motion, when presto!
even her own sex are willing to laud!

She went on.

"You know that a woman with a family, who is
also her own housekeeper, may work and work, in
her husband's house, year in and year out, without ever gaining anything in a monied way."

"Not only that," said Hetty, "but their work is not appreciated as it should be. I shall be a housekeeper to no man. In my way of thinking it does not pay as an art, for it is a great art, when well understood. But certainly, homes must be kept in order, family work must be done, and to be sure my plan would but selfishly shift the responsibility from the shoulders of the more able woman, upon those of her weaker sister. That cannot be helped. The only emollient for the case would be to so modify the system of housework so that its monotonous details and its irksome drudgery, would fall as lightly as possible upon servants and housekeepers."

In this way could the woman who had ruthlessly played fast-and-loose with her lover, theorize as to right and wrong in a domestic way; and she might, too, be good enough to carry it out in the practice of her future life, for, like a beautiful rose tree, she was not all thorn.

"Your ideas may be proper enough, yet I have, as you well know, always considered the arrangement of her home as the legitimate employment for woman," said her aunt. "Still, I begin to realize the fact that it, of itself, will not long keep the wolf from the door, that is, after all outside influences are removed as a way of income. Yet a good housekeeper is a fine thing and does seem to be the proper work for a woman, provided she could always find a support for it."

"Yes, but there is the 'provided' to get over. That is a great word in this place. The provision

is not always—indeed very often—filled, and for
that reason every woman, no matter what her
station may be, should have some sort of trade or
profession upon which she might rely in a time
of need; together with all the knowledge of busi
ness to be got at by her, and these attainments
need not interfere with her home duties."

Had Mrs. Desmond taken close notice of her
niece, when she spoke of her lover, she would
have noticed the least bit of alteration of facial expression, but she did not notice it for the reason
that she was not a close observer of anything; at
any rate not of the human physiognomy. That
was not one of her foibles. Whatever of peculiarity, this woman with her preconceived notions of
the duties and circumscribed limits of her own
sex, was possessed, the one of a quizzical impertinent look was not among them.

She never took a mental inventory of her vis-a-
vis as to his virtues and vices, his strengths and
his weaknesses, for the mere sake of her own
curious satisfaction.

Heads a many might pass before her vision without her being able to tell whether their owners
were giants of intellect, or the opposite; whether
their cranial facade ascended with the height and
regularity of an upright semi-ellipse, or whether it
was cut short like a polled hillock.

She could not, and did not, with the immovable
fixity of a Fowler, and others of his kind, settle
the question as to the ability or inability of those
upon whom she happened to set her eyes.

Perhaps all of this was to her credit, perhaps it was to her discredit, but so it was.

She bustled off to the sleeping apartment, when she had finished her talk with Hetty, where she found her husband just awakened from a fitful slumber, in which the delirium of fever had caused phantoms, the most grotesque and wild, to flit across his mind with almost lightning rapidity. He seemed to be worse than he as yet had been, so that his wife thought it advisable to call a physician to his aid.

Affairs had been going badly with the family for some time past. John, in whose name the farm rested, had been compelled to borrow money to help him out of the difficulty of making payments on machinery and other implements of farm work, and this had been the cause of a mortgage being placed upon the whole estate with the house included.

He had not prospered according to his hopes. Drouth had destroyed his crop of grain, both wheat and corn; fall rains had ruined his hay, which, along with the low price then ranging for farm produce, had nearly ruined him. Interest payments could no longer be kept up, until at length its heavy accumulations caused a foreclosure of the mortgage.

His father's failing health, too, helped along the crisis, as his assistance in a financial way was missed, he no longer being able to follow his vocation as a lumberman.

The family had been an expensive one for the

amount of income received, as Mrs. Desmond, with
her stilted ideas, would never permit her daughters
to do anything in the way of earning a penny for
themselves; nor would she allow them to do the
heaviest work of the household; so that a domestic was always kept for that purpose, whose board
and weekly wages made no small hole in their
means.

The Desmonds in the East, she said, had always
had their servants about them, and she should not
be the first to break the custom.

The place had been taken, with an offer of the
house and one acre at the price of one thousand
dollars. This from the mortgagee, out of humane
considerations, as the land was now worth a great
deal more than that, irrespective of the buildings
and improvements about the place.

The gift received from Hetty would just square
this, so that their prospect was not so dark as it
might have been, as they would yet have a roof
which they might call their own. Different it
would be, though, from the eighty acres of good
land once possessed by them. It had been acquired at a time before the great rise in real
estate, and before the rapidly swelling city had
made its encroachment near its boundaries.

It was different now as to value and had honest,
but unlucky, John made out to have steered clear
of machinery sharks, he might now have been a
rich man.

As it was there was nothing before him but to
accept the position, which he at one time had been

able to offer to others—that of laborer upon the land of some one more fortunate than himself—as farm labor would be all that he was skilled in enough to compass, not having the benefits of mechanical training of any sort.

Work of that kind could never command the wages of a skilled mechanic, so that the outlook was gloomy enough.

Poor John!

These misfortunes, along with the declining health of the only girl he had ever loved, and still loved as dearly as his own life itself; although he knew that her love was not his, but belonged to another and stronger man than himself, was rapidly converting the quiet, plodding man into a gloomy and morose misanthrope.

He still went to see Eldie, to take to her presents of fruit and of flowers, and to attend to her wants in the way of bringing paints and other materials from the city as an assistance to her artistic labors, at which she still worked with all of the force which her deceitful disease would admit.

Sunset Clouds was the title of the piece upon which she was engaging her dying powers, and, as if the inspiration of genius strengthened as her physical powers waned, the work far exceeded anything which she had heretofore accomplished; in truth was a masterpiece which the world-renowned of the profession might well have been proud to claim as their own.

How finely were the amber, the violet and the

rose, blended into one mass of softly rolling cloud upon the field of clearest blue!

John watched the work grow with pleasure and delight, for, as is sometimes the case, under his plain, undemonstrative manner, was hidden a fine vein of ideality, amounting to at least an appreciation of the elevated and the beautiful, if he was not possessed of the power to create it.

He belonged to the great class which supports' genius, for what would that divine gift amount to, if, upon the one side all were possessed of the creative faculty, or, upon the other side, all were so low in appreciative ability as to not be able to give it their recognition?

Then there was in his case the additional incitement offered by love for the fair creator of the picture, the creator whose madonna-like eyes grew in lustre and intensity of expression each day, and whose cheek grew as clear and vivid in color as the tints of her sky-scene beneath her forming brush.

The minor points of her chef de euvre were found in the soft swell of the lake waves, in the curving bank and sedgy shore where the rushes and arrow-head stood thick, as did the calla-like lilies of the Nile, when the Hebrew babe in their midst in his pitch-lined crib under the guardianship of the sad-eyed Isis, looked from their midst.

Hetty left, and the three goddesses attendant upon beauty, Aglia, Thalia, Euphrosyne went with her. Also the fairies or spirits of evil destiny, and unless she make for herself an ægis of repentance and good works, the gloom of their dark wings must always overshadow her.

Her treacherous conduct toward them in the double life she led while on her visit, to say nothing of her base ways toward Charles Lennox had left a deep stain of disgrace upon her character which time would never erase.

In time there came a letter stating the prosperous condition in which her money had placed her husband, as the head of a flourishing mercantile business in the city of Cincinatti; and of the death of her mother, whose end had been hastened by the ungrateful conduct of a daughter, upon whom every good at the command of her parents had been lavished during her childhood and youth.

Lennox had gone West, according to his intention, where he was manfully struggling to overcome the shortcomings of his early days, and with no poor success, as his natural ability began to appear, under the severe system of mental development which he had adopted for himself at the outset.

Joy had at last spread its wings over the home of the Flemmings.

The month of February, with its skies of porcelain, its softening snow and twittering bird-life of black-colored buntings; the one in which the grief of illness and of financial loss came to the Desmonds, brought to them the news of the success of one of the much abused inventions of the family head.

The prospect was that hereafter no more pinch-

ing want would be known to them, no more borrowing of money from greedy, unscrupulous
lenders, but, instead, plenty of all that makes life
bearable and happy; plenty of food, of clothing,
of pleasure, and of that which is more than all
else beside, the spirit of independence, or con-
scious ability to make one's own way in the world
without the assistance of others.

Upon the twenty-fifth of this month, across the
white expanse of prairie, a dark line of carriages
had cast their gloomy trail on their way to a
neighboring cemetery.

It was the funeral of Jaax's wife, which was following close upon the wake of his two children.
Foul air, low, stifled and filthy quarters, together
with a general hardship of life, had at last done
their work upon the poor victims of his avarice
and meanness.

A few months after this he met his friend Clip-
lip, whose business he knew as much about as
did that good man himself.   He, Jaax, made it a
point to know all of his neighbors' affairs, for, like
all persons of low mental status, he had no power
to attract unto himself, and to digest any other
knowledge which might be to him more beneficial.

"How you do?" he asked.

"I do as usual," was the answer, "but I believe
that affairs have not been going so well with you
of late."

"Vot?" you mean de dead ov mine vife?"

"Yes, dot vas von druble.   I mees her more as

de children aber. I does not long do mid oud von
oder vife. Von good vife for de work is a great
ding for a man. She help much along. Mine
vife dot I bury, she good for de work. She work
all de time. But, how is it about de match between you and Mees Shaw, eh? I guess dot she
never marry you, Clipper. You pe too slow. You
pe no pissness man."

"I have enough to attend to my own business,"
said his listener.

"Yes, put not ven you lost dot dree hundred
dollars in de land deal. I knows all about dot,"
and he gave a peculiar and intensely German
shrug to his shoulders.

"But, den, I suppose, dot money what Charley
Lennox gave you makes dot all right till you goes
vonce more on de speculation. Den avay he goes
agin."

Clipper looked in amazement.

This, of all secrets, he did not, at present, if ever
at all, wish to be made known to his acquaintances.

He had supposed a knowledge of the odd circumstances to be lodged within the breast of himself and of Lennox.

Had the latter told it?

He thought the contrary, as, upon their parting,
he had made a request of him to say nothing of
the affair, and he had given his promise accordingly.

How, then, did this mephitic imp of meddle-
someness come to know of it?

The question was beyond his power of answering.

It was one of the mysteries.

"Ha! ha! ha!" laughed his tormentor, "I find oud all apout dot pisness.₀ I finds eferyding. Dere ish alvays a vay you know."

"Some one," he considered, "must have found out through the bank in which it is deposited."

He had put it away there, with the intention to soon invest it in goods in the grocery line, and, in conjunction with an acquaintance of his, to open a small store in the vicinity. Hannah, he had wished to know nothing of the transaction until upon some fine morning her relentless dark eye would fall upon a spanking new sign board, with the name of "W. Clipper & Co., Grocers," inscribed thereon.

But here it was all out, or would be soon, for he would just as leave trust it to the four winds as to have it on the tongue of this man.

It seemed to him like a complete triumph of the meanly impertinent, over-modest, mind-your-own-business people. Indeed, to the staid and observant man it was patent that the children of Belzebub do mostly carry their point in whatsoever they undertake, be it right or wrong, while the children of rightiousness were often found coming out at the declining end of the too-to—so to speak—in order to tone down, or up rather, an exceedingly Anglo-Saxon phrase.

Whatever was the cause of this sad state of affairs he could not tell, but this he did know, that it surely ought not to be, at least, according to his way of ruminating, or according to all laws of justice.

But justice! where was it?

The thing bearing the name was but a miserable phantasm, such as the Gnostic thinks of all things. .

Real justice must have expanded its white wings and sailed away to the etherial realms of Heaven at the time of the expulsion of our first parents from the gates of paradise, never to return till the earth be changed and purified for the second habitation of regenerate man.

Were this not the case, this philosopher mused, surely this vulgar and blatant Tueton would not be able to hold the reins over him always.

Thus meditating he went across the meadow, now glorious in its May dress of green, and richly embossed by the yellow of the dandelions, the white of the anemone, the purple of the violet and red of the spring aven; where the crowfoot and saxifrage were lifting their stalks, and the larks were trilling their shrillest notes.

He reached the home of his prospective partner, who had pitched his bit of a frame house underneath the beetling brow of a bluff, which sheltered it from the north wind, as it came sweeping down the river valley with but little to break its mad fury until it reached this frame of the lake.

Samuel Jones had a wife and one child.

The last was the pest of the household in a mischievous way, the first was its pillar of strength.

Nothing did her liege lord ever so much as dream of doing without her sanction.

Good natured enough, so long as everything went according to her views, but when affairs took an opposite turn, her wrath was aroused, and in this state it was tremendous.

At such times she could, and did speak her mind, with a vim equal to her Amazonian front, and force of character. A violent outbreak of temper invariably caused the slightly one-sided knob on the end of her oddly-formed, long nose, to assume at least a barleycorn to its length, while her wide mouth would open and close with the snap and percision of an iron trap-door.

Had Clipper saw fit to, in a mental way, make a steelyard of his dislike, with Jaax upon one end and Mrs. Lennox upon the other, the balance would have been exact; as he could not tell, for the life of him, which were the more disagreeable of the two.

She had such a hateful way of obtruding her bold. visage into the affairs of others, and especially of those whom she considered shiftless, or not sufficiently worldly-minded to hold good their own in life, that made her extremely repugnant to him.

With Jones it was different.

Here he met quite a congenial soul, indeed, one who would have come up to his ideas quite well, had it not been for the fact that he allowed but too much the virago-like qualities of his wife to be felt in his affairs.

Mrs. Jones had, however, always entertained a wish to, at some time, be able to see her gentle lord established in some sort of a commercial business, even though small, with herself as principal dictator.

By dint of hard working, scraping and saving, they had managed to lay back five hundred dollars from the husband's wages as a day laborer, and what little revenue Mrs. Jones herself derived from the butter of her two cows, the vegetables of her half acre of ground and the eggs of her numerous poultry.

With this sum they proposed to join with Clipper, and his five hundred, in a business concern, which, if rightly managed, they had no doubt would realize enough for both partners to subsist independent of outside resources. Erroneous thought!

It is doubtful whether, under different circumstances, Mrs. Jones would have given her consent to the alliance, as Clipper was not in accordance with her opinion of what an energetic man of business should be, and she also doubted her husband's efficiency in that direction.

Upon the whole, the strongly calculating woman fully expected that, unless the general easiness of disposition of the two masculine members of the firm was set off by her own vigorous policy, and strength of purpose, the scheme would prove a failure. She, however, had sufficient confidence in her own abilities to allow the undertaking to progress.

She, then, met the future partner of herself and husband with a countenance quite modified in its aspect, compared with what it had formerly been upon meeting with the man whose lack of thrift was a source of contempt in her eyes; and whose quiet manner and correct speech were entirely beyond her comprehension.

"Good evening, Mr. Clipper," was her friendly salutation, as she responded to his knock, while a jerky, nervous smile spread itself from the corners of her mouth until it disappeared under her skimp, tightly drawn black hair above the swarthy brow. It left no trace behind. The face was again its hard, natural self with the sharp, shrewd look and querulous air upon it.

"We have been looking for you all of the afternoon," said Samuel, handing him a chair. "Please to sit down."

"Thank you," said Clipper, "That is just my way, I always sit down, I never sit up."

They both looked at him with good-natured surprise depicted on their faces. It seemed so strange for their visitor to indulge in a joke of any sort.

"We had almost given up your coming today. We want you to make out the bill of goods so that we may know just what our money will do," said Mrs. Jones.

Then she turned to her four-year-old offspring who was silently taking an inventory of their guest's clothing and general appearance.

"I say, Teddy (short for Edward), get out of the

way, there, and don't stand gaping like a young fool. Take a seat back yonder, on your stool."

But Teddy was not in the humor to obey. He walked sullenly out of the house and commenced to throw stones at the chickens.

"Five barrels of pork, at twelve dollars per barrel," commenced Clipper, after pen, ink and paper had been brought to him," which will be sixty dollars. Two barrels of corned beef at ten dollars per barrel, twenty dollars."

Then he mentioned sugar of different grades, molasses, tea, fruits dried and canned, butter by the firkin, lard, cheese, eggs, etc., etc., etc., the etc.'s counting more than the articles mentioned, until he was through and the one thousand dollars duly expended, its outlay likewise covering a small building, to be set upon leased ground, within the city limits, at a populated point.

When completed the bill bore upon its face so much of an air of precision, both as to cast and elaborateness of detail, that even Mrs. Jones was compelled to admit that he had done his work well.

That part of the business was quite beyond the reach of the knowledge of either her husband or herself. True, they might have been able to do a small amount of calculation; to buy and sell a small lot of any given article, but to make out a bill of cost of different quantities and qualittes, with so many of those disagreeable little things —as Mrs. Jones termed them—called fractions coming in, along with the prices thereof, was too much for their mathematical skill. "Even I," she one day said to a neighbor, in speaking of the matter, "can't see through 'em."

Of course, she mentally cogitated, nobody would expect it of Samuel, much as they might expect it of myself.

This defection on his part gave her no qualms of shame. She was not of the sort of women whose delicacy and innate generosity of heart would have caused her to wish her husband to appear in the eyes of the world as the stronger of the two. His shortcomings, in a calculating way, was something of a drawback to their financial success, and that was all that gave her any annoyance.

Oblivious of the fact, that a woman, whatever her originality or attainments may be, is yet but a woman, or the fainter, if finer, semblence of the stronger by her side; without whose support —unless it be in exceptional cases—she is altogether at rough seas, and that it is no honor to her to be more brilliant than her husband.

She hustled about to get the evening meal, and as her tongue could, and mostly did, work to the music of a pendulum—and that a fast one—she employed it upon this occassion in laying out the regulations, or principles, upon which the store was to be conducted. "I shall have no trusting out of the goods," she said emphatically, as she slapped a couple of floured mackeral, face downward into the blue smoke of the frying pan. "Once we begin to credit and we are done for. I have seen enough of that sort of work. Out go the goods, to Tom, Dick and Harry; people mostly on the lookout for some simpleton who is easy enough to credit them, but the balance for them, in money or anything else for that matter, never comes back to the poor dupe."

"What we want is to put up a picture of a dead dog, with the words, 'poor trust is dead, bad pay killed him.' That's what my uncle Timothy did, and he throve, I kin tell ye. He made a good living and laid by something for a rainy day besides. But he handled himself lively. Did all the work about the store, or shop, as he called it himself. I shall never want our place to be called a store, as shop is the right way, I am sure. Who ever says, 'lets go a storin,' they say, 'let's go a shoppin,' and that proves my way to be correct." Then she gave such a decisive shake to her head, and such a twist to the firm curve of her lower jaw that her false teeth almost lost their footing in the conflict.

The future partner of Mrs. Jones' husband eyed her askant, and listened to her voluble tongue, as she rattled her sauce-pans and dishes about, and vigorously flourished her dish-cloth.

If this was going to be the way all of the time, he thought, this Zantippe among women would drive him wild. His Hannah could talk, to be sure, but there was some sense in her discourse, a great deal in his opinion.

This woman had a little of common sense which rolled like a turbid river from her broad mouth.

There was, though, he admitted, a good deal in her talk about the credit system to be considered in their future engagement. Theoretically, she was right, at least, so far as bringing the commercial part to a successful outcome. As to the moral part, there would have to be a conflict on his belalf before he could carry out the plan.

How could his sympathetic heart bear to refuse some suffering fellow mortal the wherewithal to stave off the cravings of hunger from himself and family, perchance of helpless wee ones, when the thermometer stood at thirty or more below, on a bitter winter's day?

It would be gall and wormwood to him, he was certain.

He resolved, though, to follow Mrs. Jones' counsel in this respect, as common sense told him that, with the limited amount of capital at their disposal, it was the only safe method.

Therefore, nerve himself he would, to sell the goods upon the ready cash system only, and so be able, through the prosperity engendered by this conservative style, to give where charity was really deserved, outright, and expect nothing in return.

Let the credit system be carried on by persons more able to assume its dangerous risks. So far he meant to profit by the mouthings of this dark-browed virago, but here, he decided, her advice should cease to be taken into account.

To have a woman of her mental calibre continually over-stepping her prerogative about the

place of business would be more than even he
could endure. He would be compelled to exercise
all of his powers of resistance in order to overcome her spirit of impertinence, but it would have
to be done.

In reality Clipper's nature was about to undergo
a complete metamorphosis.

He was about to step out of the anomolous
position of that of an educated and refined man
who had never before essayed at any sort of means
to gain a livelihood, other than that which had
been pursued by his ancestors in barbaric ages, or
by the more recent aborigines of his native land,
into one of a more modern if not more respectable
color.

At length supper was announced.

" Look for Teddy, " says Mr. Jones.

"Not at all," replies his spouse, "he kin wait his
supper for this once. He's all right. I see him
now, sitting astride of the dog-house and eyeing
the ducks. Set up, Mr. Clipper, and taste some of
my home-made cheese. I pride myself upon being
the best cheese-maker in the neighborhood, Miss
Hannah Shaw not excepted."

Upon this she gave a sly but knowing look
toward her guest, who, catching the expression,
fell into such a nervous trepidation that it had the
effect of upsetting his plate into his lap! Mr.
Jones had filled it, like the bumper of Bacchus,
to overflowing, with all sorts of edibles, gravy,
potato-mash, cheese and mackerel, along with all
the culinary variety which made Mrs. Jones' teas

wear the aspect rather of a midday than an evening meal.

Clipper, poor man, was both mortified and annoyed at the catastrophe.

In vain did Mrs. Jones wash and rub with a suds
made of strong soap; the grease from the oleagin-
ous medley would not be removed, and, in consequence his best pants were spoiled.

Mrs. Jones was equally put out.

It was a most outragiously stupid piece of work,
in her thoughts.

If this man, whose future destiny was to be so
closely linked with that of her husband and herself, could admit of an accident so foolishly careless as this, what might he not do, as a veritable
son of awkwardness, in the way of tieing up parcels and other things about the place of sale?

She was more out of notion with him now than
ever.

There was her uncle, of previous citation, who
once had a clerk of so unskillful a make-up as to
always tie up his groceries after the fashion of a
sack with a string in the middle, so making them
to look like the shape of a certain fat old woman
of her acquaintance.

Besides this, he sold salt for sugar, and sugar
for salt, along with other most unheard-of mis-
takes, that complaint was loud against him; that
a peremptory dismissal was necessary to the prosperity of the establishment.

This same young man, she remembered, afterward got himself a position as boss of a lot of

wood-choppers, in the vicinity, and was one day found, in a sitting posture, with his back against a tree, and a partly whittled stick in his hand, dead!

"Died of heart disease," was the stereotyped verdict of the jury summoned.

"Died of the cuss of laziness," was her uncle's decision, with which she fully agreed.

He had died, she was certain, from sheer want of energy to keep up the necessary friction for running so complicated a piece of machinery as the human frame.

Plenty of elbow grease, was her usual saying, was what was needed as a lubricator for the joints. Physical exercise gave both strength and development.

Perhaps this fact, put into practical demonstration, was what caused the abnormal size of Mrs. Jones' jaws and mouth, as they had ever been duly exercised, both in a talking and masticating way.

About the time of the dismissal of this clerk her uncle had had his famous vision.

That was some few months before the outbreak of the war of secession, when, notwithstanding that the silver-tongued orators of the Republicans of the North had been proclaiming with circling hand the universal brotherhood and divine right of freedom of all mankind, brown, black, white and yellow; and the equally enthusiastic Democracy of both North and South, had their index finger pointed with an opposing rigidity toward the laws of slavery as set down in the old Testa-

ment as a sufficient warrantee of their cherished
institution; just as the Mormon looks to the same
source as a protection to their pet theory, yet the
mass of the people did not believe that the argument would reach the extreme alternative of taking up arms, section against section.

Secession?

Who could think of it?

Surely the people living below Mason and Dix-
on's line—those who had been of the staunchest at
the proclamation of National Independence—those
who had responded so readily at the call for volun-
teers against that uniped wretch, Santa Anna and
his dark-browed Spanish cahorts, at the war of
Mexico—those who, upon the patriot-thrilling day
of the Fourth of July, never omitted to send forth
the incense of a barbacue of ox and of possum,
while the rampant bands played the nation-stir-
ring airs of "Star Spangled Banner" and "Yankee-
doodle," would never think of a thing so treacherous.

During these asseverations and negations, then
it was that this seer-gift, a fit theme for those of
clairvoyant speculations to note with care, came
upon her uncle, Timothy Banks.

It happened in this wise, according to the old
man's vision, a version which no one saw fit to
doubt, as he was known both at home and abroad
as a person of veracity. A good deal to say among
the piney lands of Jersey, where truth is nigh
about as scarce as snow during the dog-days, or
watermelons at Christmas-tide.

He was sitting, he said, before the flaming log of a broad, old-fashioned fire-place in his country kitchen; resting his corn-afflicted toe cautiously upon the edge of the fender, while supping from a mug in his hands his usual afternoon drink of warmed cider.

Let no one possessed of asinine propensities insinuate that the cider had gotten a little too old, or that its effect had ought to do with the mental state of the narrator, as such was not the case at all.

Cosily enjoying himself, then, with no untoward outside reflections obtrusively thrusting themselves forward to mar the serenity and complacent satisfaction of his mental area, on a sudden his ears were assailed by the martial music of fife and drum coming up from the deep ravine which ran along to the east of the house.

What a strange sight met his wondering gaze!

A regiment of infantry dressed in uniform, followed by a like number of cavalrymen, marching with measured tread over the dead pine leaves and moss.

For several minutes he watched the singular proceeding, and then it vanished into thin air as suddenly as it had appeared.

From the time of the fulfillment of this optical presentment by the outbreak of the war in a short time afterward, his belief in a hereafter for the human soul and a divine care over things mundane was settled.

Before this, his view of that subject had been a peculiar one.

To him death had meant merely an invisible
infusorial migation from a habitation too diseased
for their further support, into one of a healthy
tone, where, by their own mysterious process, they
might contribute in building up a new life-form
to.take the place of the dead.

The conception though, was not his own. The
belief had been imbibed from the teachings of a
German with whom he once came in contact, and
who admitted of no God, other than the workings
of nature in its everlasting round of cause and
effect.

All of these peculiarities of her uncle Timothy,
brought about through her contemplation of him
in connection with his business abilities, flashed
across her mind with electric speed, as she
gathered up the spilled victuals and arranged
another setting of table gear for her guest.

The affair dampened the tone of convesration
considerably. Clipper had little to say, finishing
the meal almost in silence, and then left as soon
as he had made some arrangements with Jones
about the building to be used as a store.

Mrs. Jones was disappointed.

She had been broken off by this incident from a
most delicious bit of self-praise as to her abilities
as a cook, housekeeper and general manager.

Clipper wended his way, his eyes on the silent
stars, until he reached his home where he was
soon locked in the arms of Morpheus, being much
too tired to think over his future prospects.

Only until midnight though, was he allowed to

sleep, for at that hour precisely he was awakened by a party of men who were out on the look for little Ted Jones.

After Clipper left, his mother had went out to call him to supper, but he was not to be found.

In vain they searched for him, and called his name along the quiet lake, over the bluffs and among the copse of the glens, until they became so frightened that they felt it to be necessary to call to their assistance some of the neighbors.

All night the party kept up the search, and not until far on the next day did they find him, and then only to draw his half-dead body from the muck of a distant swamp, into whose miry depths he had sunk in his chase after wild fowl!

Poor child!

His form was so chilled by the wet and cold by which it had been surrounded, that it was in vain that the physician, who had been called, worked with and stimulated it. The efforts proved fruitless. A raging fever set in, and, before another day had driven the darkness from the sky, his child-life had gone out from its suffering tenement, back to its everlasting abode; the day-spring of life's fountain leaving upon the baby-face that strange look of quick transition from extreme anguish to one of glorified peace; a change peculiar to the face of the human alone, and standing isolated from all forms of brute life at this dissolution is of itself, a sufficient proof against all the sophisms of infidelity, of the divinity placed upon God's crowning work.

Spirits to mortal eyes invisible, had, no doubt, about his dying bed, waited to help the struggling young life across the dark stream of death, their beatific presence all unfelt by the coarse clay about them!

The rivers Styx and Charon, the gloomy boatman of the black-draped barge, the mystic legends of Druid-life, were but the rude conceptions of the true scenes which are enacted at the last supreme moment of life, or the forerunner of the modern belief of angelic aid to the passing spirit.

The child was buried amidst a profusion of flowers, brought to the mourning parents by the hands of sympathizing friends, and from that time Mrs. Jones' temperament was considerably modified in its severity, when compared with her former self.

True, the termagant tongue would sometimes break out as of yore in vituperation or harsh invective against some fancied or real enemy, or some patent wrong, but this was only upon rare occasions. Her general tone of conduct was characterized by more of a consideration for the feelings of others; more of a spirit of charity and peace with those around her, for beneath all her coarseness of nature there beat the mother's heart, and that heart had been touched by the chill finger of death, the great softener of character.

A few months after these events, the astute old German, Jaax, brought to his home a new wife in the form of a Swedish widow and her three children.

"A goot vife to worruk, and very sthill," he told
one of his neighbors, after the wedding. "She
yusht worruks right on, un say nodings. Ash to
de childrens, day pe all poys, un I makes it all
right mit dem. I prings dem up to good worruk.

He evidently considered the proceeding quite a
scheme to help him to get on in the world.

He placed women precisely as does the tenth
commandment, "Thou shalt not covet thy neighbor's wife, nor his ox!" Here she is on a parallel
with the cattle, and there is no counter-poising
command as to the woman to not covet her neighbor's mate. They were not supposed to be sufficiently tainted by the fall of the Edenic pair for
that, or else they were simply ignored the rights
of the human, as given to the masculine genus.

Love!

Jaax loved his wife just as the brute does its
mate. Nothing less, nothing more.

Not long did Major Stewart allow his Anna to
drudge in the factory, for one day a wedding party,
consisting of her father and mother, her brother
John and her sister Anna, along with Robert
Orme, drove down to the city where the couple
were united in the bonds of matrimony; made
holy by the faith which each placed in its vows,
together with a firm determination to follow out
this pledge, to their life's end through evil as well
as good.

Then he took her to a snug little home which
he had already bought and furnished, in which it
is to be presumed that they will, after the fashion

of all good people, live in peace and contentment, each believing the other the best of all the world beside, never to allow the face of another to come between them, nor no adverse circumstances to mar their "land of Beulah."

Abraham and Sarah, Isaac and Rebecca, together with all good couples who have lived since marriage was instituted, should be their models.

Alienation and the divorce court should be unknown to them.

"Flesh of my flesh and bone of my bone," should not be a mere hypothesis, but real.

What a pity it is that all couples cannot be so mated!

A state of such universal bliss perhaps is not, in the nature of the degenerate race of mortals, to be admitted.

The devil must get in his oar somewhere, and he finds no more inviting flood for this navigating piece of furniture, than the wide sea of matrimony.

How he does love to set agog a family disturbance!

To tell the man or woman, who may happen to be possessed of more balloon than ballast, or, in other words, with more of romance than of common sense in their mental make up, that they have met with an affinity outside of the marriage bond.

That the partner, who perchance has faithfully toiled by their side for years; sharing both sorrow and gladness, is to be lightly set aside in order to gratify the most whimsical fancy, inspired by some new face or form, not, perchance, so worn or aged as the one who has poured out their best blood and spirit in the struggle for the sake of the disloyal companion.

What a pandemonium would he, of the cloven foot, fain create, could he only be able to bring about the general belief, that no two were ever made to go through the journey of life together, and that the command, concerning the marriage union, given in Paradise is of no effect.

Resist him and he will flee.

His machiavelian presence, though gifted with far more craft to impose upon his weak victims than ever was brought to bear by that renowned esquire, Sancho Panza, against his unsuspecting master, Quixote, may yet be overcome here, as in all of the other affairs of life.

That human tread-mill, the factory of Dentwell & Co., is in full operation. From the lowest tier of workers, up to the highest, all are busy, for the season is one of unprecedented prosperity to the firm.

Overworked some of the operators certainly are.

Their pale faces and slow steps, which have none of the bouyant elasticity of youth, plainly tell the fact.

Yet these symptoms may not altogether proceed from this cause. Wages inadequate to meet the demands of life, and, in some cases, burdens of domesticty laid upon shoulders too young to bear up under the load; or, it may be, that family sor-

· row has laid its hand upon youthful cheeks, robbing them of their bloom.

Among those who, either through successive gradations have arisen to a superior position, or else have received it through some outside influence, might be seen the shapely head, covered by its weath of light hair, the innocent blue eyes and fresh complexion of Sarah Desmond.

Her position in the factory as a paper folder was given to her at her first entrance to the place, upon a vacancy, just then at hand, coupled with a deference to her appearance and bearing, which were somewhat different from most of the girls.

Envy is sometimes—indeed very often—excited in the breasts of operatives; toward those who undeservedly hold situations, in their thought, above them.

Girls who, were strict justice given to them, should long ago have left their irksome stand at the not over-clean rag barrels, where is made the assortment of the contents which is needful before they can be converted into paper by the wheels of the hungry machinery.

In this respect Sarah was an exception, Her unassuming modesty and nameless grace of manner, had won all hearts towards her from the very first; from the impulsive, warm hearted daughter of Erin to the finely fibered, impressive sister from the sea-washed coast of Scandia.

It must then have also been these qualities along with her purity and unconsciousness of evil in the world, that gave to her an attractiveness in the eyes of the junior partner of the firm.

Certainly, it was not any particular claim to beauty which might be made for her. Her form was too spare, her face and features too expressionless, yet to the blase roue she was possessed of a charm different from that of which belonged to the ordinary woman of the world, as she is met in society.

He was tired of that stereotyped class, and determined to seek in pastures new, food for his erratic desires.

Therefore he commenced to work with all of the powers of his fascination upon the simple minded country girl, who until now, had never met the man to make her heart to thrill in his presence.

What was it that caused her face to blanch, and her eyes to drop beneath his gaze?

Nothing else than that mysterious force called magnetism, electric force mesmeric power, or by any biologic name, or spiritual name by which one mind is made to feel the power of another.

Walter Vernon was possessed of this force in a remarkable degree, and was as proud of it, and as fond of exerting its influence as it is possible for any man to be who is inordinately vain of all that pertains to himself, and soon had the satisfaction of knowing that in her unsuspecting innocence she would be in his hands, as is wax to the worker, and as easily moulded to his purpose.

The way was easy.

Notwithstanding the strong efforts which have

been made by lovers of justice for the equalization of the sexes, there yet remains a wide social hiatus between the fallen man and the fallen woman. The fallen man may arise, in fact is, very often, not even considered as being at all down, and if so, a hundred hands, both strong and fair, are outstretched to assist him once more to his feet.

But to the woman no such lot is, as yet assigned.

There is but one way, really, to give justice in this matter, and that would be to make as legally the unmarried mother and her offspring, claimants of the protection and property of the seducer, as those who hold the claim according to law.

To be sure, wrong would sometimes occur in this way, but would it equal in injustice and crime production, the system of the present?

Under such conditions the insinuating scoundrel, either married or single, would be extremely loth to add to his encumbrances as a family man; so that the weakness or destitution of women would no longer afford on undefenceless prey upon which to gratify their base passion.

Vernon did not fear.

He never intended to become the husband of Sarah Desmond any more than he had his victims before her. Therefore, it was with no especial compunctions of conscience, that he sent her home to her mother just eighteen months after her entrance into the factory, with a check for one hundred dollars in her hand; and in one month afterward she became a mother.

Where was Vernon?

He disappeared for awhile, until he heard by means of a private detective that the Desmonds, not believing in such measures, meant to institute no legal proceedings against him. Then he came back as great a favorite in society as ever!

A few whispers as to his late escapade in crime were heard, but little attention was given to them. The man was rich, and that, like the charity of scripture, covers a multitude of sins.

Poor Mrs. Desmond! What a sorrow was this for her proud nature! What could she do?

With all of her unmerciful opinions toward a woman who so far forgot the dignity due to herself as to listen to the breathings of unlawful love, and when this woman was her own child!

The mother's love within her asserted itself, however, with a lion's strength. Excuses many urged themselves upon her in defense of the miserable creature who really deserved pity.

Had she not kept her too much in ignorance of the ways of the world, through that very pride which was so much wounded?

Had not her antique views in regard to the retiring manners of young girls fashioned them too much after the way of medieval damsels, whose only prerogative was to marry, and by this act so assimulate with the personality of the man, that an idea above that of the animal one of maternity, and a care for her household; with as little of an outside perspective as the mole exerts in his blind burrowings; was considered as unworthy of the delicacy of her sex.

When, although considered as far too frail and flower-like to partake in any of the more elevating and spirited affairs of life, was yet ever considered as strong enough to oversee or perform all of the details of domestic drudgery, and in some countries even to guide the plough!

Glorious consistancy of man!

There was no protest against the fair creatures becoming too masculine or too labor-burdened!

Social ideas were in those times fixed.

Mankind made them and womankind assented.

Who ever was bold enough to connive at innovation, then?

Mrs. Desmond had allowed her mind to become so wrapped up in this mist of past ages, that her girls had gone out into the world more like the finely petaled flower of the hot-house than the rose, whose beauty and fragrance is strengthened by the winds and showers of outdoor life.

When too late she considered over this. To be sure, her other daughter was well settled, but not every girl has her pathway to run into so smooth a groove as that of her Anna. When it does not, what then?

Best it is for them all to be so nurtured, as to be able to meet life in all of its varied phases, both good and bad, just as their brothers are taught to do.

The humbug of their being of a mould different from the opposite sex should be left to mildew among the pages of Macpherson and others, until it exploded from the gas of its own noxiousness.

Let poetry have its full sway, only let it not make a sentimental unreality stand for truth.

The business scheme of Jones & Clipper progressed.

Relieved from the officiousness of Mrs. Jones, the work went forward under the directions of the whilom fisherman, exclusively; his partner contenting himself by obeying orders, he—unlike his wife—being far-seeing enough to note in the placid-mannered man a capacity for business, of which neither of them were possessed, and so allowed him to have his own way.

The building was erected quite large enough to suit their purpose, with an L at one side to be used as a packing room. Then their goods were judiciously selected, bought and arranged in so satisfactory a manner to Mr. Jones that he insisted upon Clipper's name being used as the leading one of the firm, deferentially putting himself in the background, as a matter of course; so that the sign was swung out with the marking, "Clipper & Jones, Grocers."

Mrs. Jones was inclined to find fault with the arrangement, but was persuaded into silence by her husband, who pointed out to her the fact that it was due to the organizing power of the principal that things had advanced in so fine a way with them.

The man was rapidly developing into quite an active person under the exciting guidance of an inciting motive.

So quietly had their movements been kept that

few knew of the enterprise, until they were fairly launched upon the world of business in their small way.

Hannah was among the number who did not know who was the proprietors of the new store, and she never once so much as dreamed that her lover was master of sufficient pluck to engage in anything of that sort, so that a day or so after the opening, as she went down to get for herself some tea and sugar, what was her surprise, upon opening the door, to meet face to face with her would-be-husband, all spick and span in a new and fashionably made suit of clothing, his shirt front shining in immaculate whitness, his hair trimmed and combed, according to the latest style, and his face beaming with pleasure, a feeling no doubt produced by a knowledge of the wonder in which he knew she would be surprised.

To be sure she was taken aback for an instant. Then her quick eye took in the surroundings.

Everything was scrupiously clean, and neatly arranged, from the few barrels of vegetables in one corner, to the boxes of sugar and cans of fruit upon the shelves; the latter partly empty ones, according to suggestion made by Mrs. Jones, who remarked that they "would help to fill up the place, and also give a look for an outlay of goods where there really was none."

Shrewd Mrs. Jones!

The poetic instinct, of at least one member of the firm, was shown by a vase of flowers, columbine, bellwort, painted-cup and phlox, interwoven with the delicate leaves of fern and meadow-rue.

"Why, William Clipper," were Hannah's first words, "I am surprised to meet you here."

"Well, I am here, and what is more, I am here to stay."

"Got a clerkship, have you?"

"A clerkship? No, I am more than that; I am senior member of this place, as your own eyes would have told you had you looked over the door as you came in. Clipper & Jones is what you would have seen there."

"Well, I did'nt look up. I hardly ever do. I am not a star-gazer, if you are. But however, William, did you manage to rise in this sort of a way? Everything, too, looks so tidy, and I declare you have got quite a stock of goods. I heard up our way about the new grocery store to be started by the Jones's; but, sakes alive, I never expected to find you here."

The little woman stepped back a pace or two and gazed upon his altered appearance. He really looked almost a handsome man, with his high pale forehead, his dark hair, mild features and soft hazel eyes.

The change had quite an effect upon Hannah.

Instead of despising him, as of old, the first thought that came to her as she contemplated the difference in his *modus vivendi*, was, that perhaps he had gone out of her reach entirely, and, with the strange inconsistency for which the little palpitating lump of flesh, called the human heart is noted, she now as ardently longed to be sued by her ascending amarosa as she formerly rejected his offers. .

With wonderful mental celerity she summed up the possibility, that the case might, hereafter, stand between them upon a plane with one of those musty old fables, belonging to people of a past age; people who were so skillful in boiling down wisdom until it could be thus carried about in lettered chunks, that modern humanity as if doubtful of its ability to do likewise, hangs with the . grasp of a Hercules, and in which Clipper would dangle high up—figuratively speaking—after the fashion of a most tempting bunch of grapes, no longer wild, but tame ones; and Hannah herself would be as a most disconsolate, but of course, artfully repudiating fox of the feminine gender.

As if quite exhausted at the thought, and in apparent forgetfulness of the past dignity, she seated herself in one of the two chairs which had been left in the place, notwithstanding the strict injunction of Mrs. Jones to allow of no seats, as an inducement to loafers who might be inclined to sit around spinning fish stories; something which would certainly have been quite inappropriate, considering the past vocation of the principal.

Quick as thought, Clipper was around the end of the counter and seated beside her in the remaining chair.

Now a great deal of the disdain of former times had left the worthy spinster's mind, therefore she stood her ground better than might have been expected.

"Well, my dear—here she blushed like a peony, and threw up her head, defiant like, as if the old spirit of trifling was coming back to her— I was to come up to your house this evening to talk over my affairs, but as you have quite opportunely dropped in I suppose this place will be as good as any to again make a marriage proposal to you. You can see for yourself"—here she broke him off suddenly—"Yes, I see that I am not going to be courted in this fashion. What? Do you think that I am gawk enough to come to you when I want any courting done?"

"There, now, Hannah," he said, mischievously, "you have owned that you do want some courting done. That is just as I expected."

Then she wrathfully pushed back her chair a pace, but her lover gave his a hitch in pursuit, and again was beside her. He had at last gotten the upper hand of his flinty-hearted charmer, as his observation taught him, and he determined to keep it.

"You insulting man, you," she hurled spitefully at him, "how dare you to so address me, Hannah Shaw, a woman whose name has never been lightly spoken of. But that only proves what a wretched set you men all are! It is my opinion that if about one-half or more of you were thinned out the world would be the better for it!"

"Well, Hannah, I'm not very particular any more, as to whether I marry or not. I am convinced that a woman is at best, an awkward sort of crea-

ture, almost too much for one man to manage, and
still not enough for two; and that her tongue, like
the revolver that no one knows is loaded, is apt
to go off at any unexpected moment, throwing its
electric shots right and left. Still, if you are willing to marry me why I am willing to marry you,
if for nothing else than the sake of keeping up
old friendship; only, remember, this is the last
time that I shall ask you. A refusal now will end
the affair between us. Shall it be yes or no?"

Hannah was in a predicament.

She really loved him more than she had ever
done. "Jog-along-straight," had ever been her
motto, and surely this seemed a little, if not a
good deal out of the common course of decorum.

That she, Miss Hannah Shaw, should not be
duly sought out and engaged in her own little
parlor, instead of in this store where she had so
inadvertantly come to her lover, seemed, in her
straight-laced way of looking at affairs, as quite
away from the eternal fitness of things.

Another slight hitch of her chair backward, followed by an equal one on the side of Clipper.
Then he seized her hand and asked again, "Yes, or
no, Hannah?"

"Yes," she jerked out spasmodically, while she
endeavored to withdraw her hand, but he held it
tightly while he fumbled in his pocket and at last
produced a plain ring of gold, which he placed
upon the engagement finger.

He had bought it the day before for the very
purpose.

She loosed her hand and sprang to her feet. He also arose and clasping her tightly to his bosom pressed a kiss upon either of her two cheeks.

"There," she said giving him a forcible push, "I have always declared that no creature so nasty as a man should dare to kiss me! Let it be the last time." Then she blushed like a peony, while Clipper smiled blandly.

At that moment a tee-tee-tee, followed by a loud guffaw was heard at the door, and in waddled Jaax, his rotund, beer-bloated form fairly convulsed with laughter. He had been witnessing the whole transaction through a side window.

He fell over a peck of onions in his boisterous hilarity, sending them flying all over the floor, while he rolled about like a porpoise, unable for some time to regain a sufficient control of his risible faculties, to gather himself up into a standing posture once more.

Hannah slipped out of the door as quickly as possible, but Clipper had to bear up under the fire of good humored raillery, which his pestiferous acquintance of old saw fit to pour upon him.

"Got her at last, I see, Glibber. Vat I told you? Yusht so soon ash you shange your peesniss you pe able to git one vife. Ha! ha! ha!" and he laughed as loudly as before.

"Put now you musht set up de lager."

"No," said Clipper, "I shall not step from the store to enter a saloon with you, but here are some cigars."

At this moment Jones came in and the old German went out.

Where during all of the time which has been devoted to other characters was Agnes Flemming? She was still living under the roof of Monsieur De Ivry.

The winter following her incarceration, as the attendant upon her mistress and friend, had been passed either in the confined atmosphere of the sick room with its monotonous cares or else suffering from the onerous attentions of Flavious Lambert, a miserable, broken-down devil of a far-away-cousin of De Ivry. He had once owned an estate near St. Cloud, another at that charming resort of the Netherlands, Ostend, together with quite an amount of plate; but not a franc of it remained. It was all lost at the gaming tables of Monaco, and he had now but a small yearly stipend allowed to him, through the generosity of an aunt, upon which to subsist.

He spent his time principally along with his dog and his gun, a veritable Nimrod, whose chief delight was in scouring over the downs and meadows lying back of the estate, so as to be able to return at nightfall with his game-bag well filled with either teal, canvass-back or partridge, as a trophy of his success as a marksman.

He would have had Agnes to marry him with nothing to build a home and to keep the wolf from the door but the bit of a stipend, and the fruits of his hunting expedition; but she refused.

Toward spring, Madame Du Boise grew very

much worse, so much worse indeed that it was
apparent to all, especially to herself, that her end
was near.

She desired the presence of an attorney, to
whom she dictated a will; leaving to Agnes the
bulk of her property, and the remainder to her
cousin at Ville De Avery, and a few days after the
soul of the eccentric woman took its flight to the
realms of the unknown spirit-land; and upon a
dreary April day, when the misty rain fell in
sweeping torrents, and the wind sighed dismally
among the beeches and oaks, her body was carried
to its last repose, over the soggy road and through
the rumbling streams, each stream with a sym-
phony distinct from the others as any listening
ear may note.

The mourners were few, but after the burial in
an obscure corner of a Parisian cemetery, by the
side of her child, Agnes planted over them rose-
mary, box and myrtle, and then had the two graves
marked by a handsome marble stone, and so left
them in unvisited solitude until the trump of the
resurrection morn shall call them forth.

After this Monsieur De Ivry had the cottage and
its grounds converted into money, which he
passed into the hands of Agnes, the value of all
chattel goods going to Madame L'Hommechapeau
and, in accordance with a wish framed by him
from the first, which was to prove for himself the
identity of his artist granddaughter across the
ocean, he at once commenced to make prepara-
tions to accompany Agnes to her home.

It took time, though.

Several months were necessary before his affairs could be arranged and placed in the hands of persons competent to care for them, and before the chateau and its grounds, together with the plantation adjacent, could be properly tenanted.

This delay was borne by Agnes quite cheerfully, much as she longed to see her friends, as the prospect of her aged friend being an accompaniment was quite a compensation for the tedium endured.

By the first of August, everything pertaining to his business had been satisfactorily shaped, and they took their departure for America, the Monsieur, accompanied by a garde du corps, as it were, in the form of a stalwart Piedmontese serving-man, and, Agnes, free to take care of herself—not even the parrot going along with her, to annoy her by his eternal noise and chatter as she left him with the house-keeper at the chateau.

The girl was, as may be imagined, in the happiest of moods, as the conveyance which carried them to the steamer on the Seine rolled through the sandy roads and over the heated plains, surrounded by the hazy, slumberous atmosphere, with its fragrance of amber pears, red-cheeked peaches, golden apricots and purple grapes.

France! Homely and sterile enough in some of her parts, yet, taken as a whole, she is wondrously rich in scenic effects, and in that quality of attractiveness which causes her sons and daughters to cling to her; if but in memory alone, and in dreams

to visit her fruitful slopes and sun-kissed vine-
yards, though oceans roll between them.

It was also during the first week of August that
Clipper and Hannah were united.

The marriage took place at a village some miles
distant, whose early name was a most harmonious
one in the softly-flowing Chippewa tongue,
but which has been changed through personal
ambition to perpetuate a family name into one far
less euphonious.

Here they drove, accompanied by quite a retinue
of friends, the procession numbering several carriages, after the fashion of old times decades ago,
in rural parts of the East.

It was the way all of her people before her had
done, Hannah said, and looked something like
having things right. None of your sneaking off
alone to some minister's house, there to be yoked
together with as little of ceremony as if the transaction which is to govern one's future life, should
be balanced as lightly as is the selection and purchase of a new gown!

At their time of life, too, the event seemed to
call for additional attention, inasmuch as it is
really, or ought to be a most worthy affair. Persons then but commence to understand themselves aright, and moreover, up from the level of
merely sensuous passion, they have reached the
elevated plain of that placid love which has for its
foundation and fabric, experience at least, and it
may be supreme moral or intellectual development; things of which the thoughtless, ardent

flame of young love takes but little note. Also in
the decline of life is really the time when the
companionship of wedlock is the most needed, she
reasoned.

The day upon which these long-courting lovers
had fixed for their bridal trip, was all that heart
could desire, with the late summer air in its
dreamy stillness resting over isle, river-valley and
uplands, and the goddess Ceres, with her wealth
of golden corn and wheat. After alighting in
front of the tiny chapel, they entered under a
light, from the small but richly stained windows,
as dimly religious as any of the great poets sing
about, and as mellow as ever came from cloistered
abbey or grey cathedral.

Then the bride and groom stood before the surpliced minister, the first in a dress of amber silk,
in trimmings of black lace, unrelieved by ornament except a single spray of golden rod at the
throat; her hair, for once allowed to be loosed
from the stiff Greek knot at the back of her head,
and allowed to be fixed in a soft coil, which, in its
abundance, formed a crown of brown, imparting
to her head a new grace. The groom wore a suit
of black, and looked pale and grave as if he felt
the importance of the step about to be taken.
They were being united under the Episcopal form
of marriage, by which so many have made their
vows, as it comes sounding down from the ages of
the dim past, since St. John and his followers
first planted the glorious liturgy in the isles of
the west, long before Augustine came with his

monks and the cross of Rome. Then the benediction was pronounced over their devoted heads,
and—congratulations over—the party left the
chapel and went to the cluster of houses grouped
along the roadside in one of which a public house
—they were to have their wedding dinner.

Such a dinner!

A feast fit for the Gods!

It was more than that!

No banquet of Egypt, Greece or Rome, in the
palmiest days of their ancient glory, could equal a
good substantial meal of modern days. Conditions were wanting to make out the parallelism.

Nectar and ambrosia! could they be at all compared with some of our present luxuries?

And the divinities, who were they?

Not half as good as Clipper and Hannah.

They had too much of either love, hatred, jealousy or envy about them for that.

Their feasts were generally held to Bachus and
Semele; this one was sacred to Gough and
Willard.

After dinner the whole party strolled out and
down into the concave, formed between the bluffs,
a veritable dell of streamlets, waterfalls, islands
and capes, formed and surrounded by the serpent-
ine windings of a creek and its branches, a home
of the naiads or water nymphs; a place for the
blessing of Arethusa herself to rest, as she views
the fairy sprits flying among the crystal white of
the foam or the silvery mist of the tossing spray
as it leaps to the vale, covered as it is by oak, lin-

den, ash and poplar, overtopping in their giant
height and circling arms the undergrowth of witch
hazel, sumach, elder and willow, with their tangle
of vines, grapes, bitter-sweet, creeper and brier,
joining all together in their twining embrace with
a clasp as firm as the serpents of the Tycoon, so
bringing them all into a general brotherhood; from
the lowliest shrub or weed struggling for light
and life in the density of its surroundings to the
stateliest tree of them all.

A great diversity of coloring there was not.

August is not the month for a variation of
dyes.

Purple and golden are the usual tints and these
were seen everywhere, in the stiff-leaved, thick-set
clusters of the pucoon, in the blunt-topped spikes
of the one-petaled amorpha, and in the delicate
swinging bells of the primrose, and the hanging
flowers of the gerardia.

Scarlet scarcely appears except where some
clinging vine of Virginia creeper is flushed here
and there in its palmete leaves with a blush,
brought through the struggle between the faintest
borean breeze and the zephyr from southern lands
with the scent of the tropics upon its wings. The
love of the tendriled twiner is for the last, for has
she not warmed the tender shoots of spring time
and helped the sun's rays to supply the wine of
life to stem and leaf, so suffusing them with green
—animating green—the color of nature's resurrection?

How the amber sunlight dances and quivers

over all, checkering the grassy carpet in a thousand forms.

And the birds!

Here, far up near the top of an oak a great eagle, with its dun-grey color and white head, is silhouetted against the sky as it perches far out on a limb, free from branches and obscuring leaves; and looking down with its yellow iris, in silent contemplation of what it deems intruders upon its natural domain.

An oriole has hung her oddly-built nest from the branch of a spreading bass until it swings far out over one of the streams, and the hawks, robins, thrushes and jaybirds have their homes everywhere, on tree and shrub, but they are silent. No trills of Spring melody now. The work of Summer has made them too tired for that. Great families have been brought into being and reared since then, and now they are almost as devoid of song-music as the wabbling turtle, the creeping eft or the gliding serpent beneath them.

High up on the crest of a bluff, whose scarred top sweeps backward for many an acre, a tangled unpruned orchard of plum looks down, the trees gnarled and grey with age, their lichened trunks and horny knots telling of a time, perchance, when none but the red man disturbed these mystic shades, as he strolled in pursuit of game, or with quiet, measured dip sent his canoe among the tall rice stalks to gather from them their wealth of food. His wigwam was here, too, as it was a favorite spot for deer and fish, as well as a place where the manes of their dead might fondly visit, with all of its charm of the works of the Great Spirit.

Would any one believe that the Hamlet in its repose among the wilds of nature as weird and dreamy as the scenes over which Isis and Osisis presides in the witching land of the lotus and the lily, the ibis and the bulbul, is almost, or quite as old—dating from its first white inhabitants—as is the stirring city whose distant hum floats upward upon the river's waves until it reaches its ears? Even so it is.

The wedding party enjoyed the surroundings much.

To Clipper the scenes were nothing new.

He had been accustomed to their beauties since early manhood.

Here he had caught many a fine haul of pickerel, or of bass, snared many a rabbit, and shot many a fowl. He said little of this for Hannah's sake.

There were, however, other interesting topics of which he could, and did talk.

On a bit of a knoll toward the south of the hollow, he could designate the spot where in days past a wayside tavern had hung its sign.

Those were in the territorial days of Minnesota, when railroads and their accompaniments of engine and coaches were unknown, and instead of the shrill whistle of the first, the not unmusical sound of the bugle of the stage-driver was heard; and for the present air-cutting speed to travelers, there was the slower and safer one of the rolling and swinging vehicle, with its comfortable cushions and its double span of horses.

Those were the palmy days for the country innkeeper.

He could then gather in the shekels by the peck, and even amass a fortune at his calling, if he managed his business aright.

Such a place had been this old home of the public, with its well kept table and its bar, where genuine old rye whisky was always to be found, and generally the juice of the vine, and brandy too, but the beer of the festive German was unknown then.

Gambling was sometimes allowed in the less reputable of these houses, but whether the foul practice was ever admitted to these fair precincts is unknown.

A child once found a piece of old silver coin while playing among these ruins. It had upon one of its faces a portrait of one of the Georges of England.

Clipper heard of it, and afterward spent several days in digging about the place in hopes of striking a deposit of treasure.

This was in the days before he knew exactly in what shape his fortune was to come to him. It was different with him now, but he remembered the circumstances well, and remembered too, that his efforts had been in vain; and that after the unfruitful work was abandoned he had been compelled to sell some of his fishing impliments in order to get something to keep him from starving, on account of his lost time.

He kept this incident of his life to himself, but told about the flight of the frightened settlers from the north during the time of the Indian outbreak—at the war of the rebellion—when the adjacent highway was strewn with cast-off luggage, in the way of clothing and all sorts of household and farm implements, as they were cast from the over-burdened fugitives in order to facilitate their speed toward the seat of refuge further on.

Also, he could point to the spots where various house-burnings had taken place; where a murder had been perpetrated in an old house, still standing, and that, in consequence, it was held by believers in the supernatural as being haunted.

So the day wore away and evening brought them home again, where, in the gathering twilight, they all saw the bride and groom enter their cottage home, a happily united couple at last.

CHAPTER XI.

Mr. Desmond is a confirmed invalid, and his wife has laid aside much, if not all, of the pride and folly of her former life, and with as brave a spirit as is compatable with one of her mind and age, is meeting the stern realities of her situation.

John, silent, patient man that he is, gives all that is possible from his slender wages to the support of his parents and sister.

The last, though is no incumbrance.

She works faithfully for the support of herself and son, the beautiful child of her misfortune, to whom she has given the Latin name of Guido, but that of Dolorose would, perhaps, be more fitting his birth and fatherless condition.

And the girl herself?

Must she, in her absinthine sorrow, like the woman of the "Scarlet Letter," go through life in social separation as a perpetual repentance for this one sin, which, as a woman not too impure for motherhood, has so visibly branded her before the world?

Her seducer is free from all that can mark him, personally, and yet, who can, with any degree of sincerity affirm, that his sin was not the greater of the two?

A man may sin and sin, with all of the impunity

of a Judah, and yet in all of the righteous indignation which that worthy displayed in his orders as to Tamar when he wished her to be punished for precisely the same offense which he had committed; they will not now, being able to quite reach the horror of the good old Jewish law, set her aside in their search for a companion through life, as altogether too debased to be classed along with their own good selves!

Robert Orme had, within the two years since which he was first introduced in these pages, made rapid advance in his scholastic ways, had received his symbol of completion in the form of a graduating diploma, leaving the university in high honor.

What was to be his pursuit in life?

Like many another bright youth, he hardly knew which way to turn in order to earn enough for his support, and found that his career at school, however successful it had been, was but the primal or initiating step upon the ladder of life, from which he must with unceasing effort climb, if he wished to attain unto anything worth the naming.

His fine poetic instinct would scarce bring his salt in a utilizing or monied way, unless he should select for himself the very arduous and slowly ascending one of literature.

True it was that his deep love of nature and her works would stand as monitors to guide and keep him in a refined state of manhood, in whatever calling he might follow, but that would be their moral, not their material, force; and if nothing else were sought after but what they could bring, his life would be that of another Clipper, a state he did not exactly care about, much as he esteemed his old friend.

As he was planning, re-planning, and digesting his plans, and casting about in order to see what trade or profession would be the best adapted to his natural bent of mind word came that Agnes Flemming was on her way home; indeed, was expected to arrive soon, and that with her was a foreign nobleman, who would claim the Janneaux as kin, also that she had been made rich through the death and will of the eccentric woman in whose care she left her home!

At first the rumor was discredited, but when it was told by the Flemmings themselves, people began to believe it, and this belief was verified, when in a week after the report got abroad, the travelers actually appeared among them. Monsieur De Ivry was quite feeble and worn out by his journey, but Agnes was changed from the sallow faced, angular girl into a blooming woman, with Ionic grace displayed in every curve of her lissome form.

Young Orme was seized with a fit of love at first sight, and it was not long before the object of his affections gave him encouragement to suppose that the passion was reciprocal.

Love hastened his decision as to a pursuit, and he fixed upon that of a civil engineer, in the employ of an uncle of his, with the promise from Agnes that she would marry him soon as his apprenticeship was over.

Mr. and Mrs. Clipper gave a party to a small circle of friends shortly after their connubial settlement, among which were her old acquaintances, Mrs. Fairchild, Mrs. Babbit, Mrs. Finch and Mrs. Weston, along with their husbands, and Mr. and Mrs. Jones.

None of the Desmonds were invited.

Hannah never did like Mrs. Desmond, although she pitied her in her family griefs and was mad enough at the man who had wrought the ruin of Sarah to have "torn him into pieces," to use her own form of expression.

Her manner of speaking ever partook more of the blunt, but forcible gothic style, than it did of the smooth but less definite Latin type, for the reason that she was all northern, and the myrids of generations through which her blood had filtered, finding their home always among the bald crags and wild glens of a mountain country where the rude winds of long winters shook their snow wreaths over all, had left as a matter of philosophical fact, these traits of their natural surrounding impressed upon their very souls.

Good strong people, but possessed of none of the willowy grace of form, and gently accented speech, which characterize the people who partake more of the rich sensuous and alluring scenes of tropic climes.

Hannah literally meant all that she said.

She could have annihilated the father of Sarah's child without any compunctions of conscience, and, although rather of the catheristic order herself, yet she had quite a good deal of charity for the young girl whose sin was one of weakness, rather than that of a depraved heart.

"If," as she used to say, "God in His goodness gave to me more of strength and of prudence than some of my sisters in the human family are possessed of, it is no reason why I should look down upon others who are not so well favored."

For the designing wretch of a man in the case she had no mercy whatever.

The child she really loved.

She had met his mother several times with him in her arms, and she so fancied him that she would have adopted him as her son, only Sarah would not part with him.

She told this to her guests, on the day of the party, in a confidential sort of way, as the pros and cons of the Desmond family were flying among them right and left in all directions.

Mrs. Fairchild, who had but little sympathy for any of them, except John, and not coinciding with Mrs. Clipper in her easy letting-down of Sarah and her fault, had, with the assistance of several others after they had dissected, probed, wrenched and twisted their reputation with tongues of double-edged severity, finally laid them out as dead without hope of resusitation through the scathing they had gotten.

Evidently the passing of the years instead of abating was increasing her love of gossip and of truculent scandal.

Then they turned to the Janneaux.

"I suppose," said Mrs. Babbit, "that the Janneaux are quite proud of their new arrival from across the seas. That odd looking waiting man who came along with—with—let me see, what is his name?"

"De Ivry," said some one.

"Oh yes, De Ivry."

"What a nice sounding name it is. Well, this man of his was up past our house riding upon a fine black horse. A new horse, none of Janneaux old crow-baits. Some one told me that the Monsieur keeps a turnout of his own. I believe he is an invalid and needs it to take his airings.

"Has any one seen him?" queried Mrs. Weston.

No one had except Mrs. Clipper. She had been down to see Eldie.

"What sort of looking man is he?" asked Mrs. Fairchild of Hannah.

"O, I didn't look much at him at all. Of course he speaks no English, so no one attempted to introduce him to me. I did notice, though, that he was quite good looking for an old man, and had a grand air about him."

It is rumored that he is rich in France, and has a fine castle and lands there, I believe it came from the Femmings," said Mrs. Finch. They say that Eldie is the daughter of his daughter who ran away from her home along with a miserable poor young artist, who, strange to say, was the brother of old Mr. Janneaux. I don't see where the artistic taste could come in along with his family. Fine conceptions of the beautiful in nature. With him they end in the size and strength of his horses, along with their ability to masticate oats.

"He is not to blame for his want of taste," said Mrs. Weston, "and as to his admiration for his horses, he is just right, they being to him a support for himself and family. But it was different with this brother of his who eloped with the Madameselle, who afterward became the mother of Eldie and Camille. He, so Mrs. Janneaux told me, was really a genius in his line; one who, although belonging to the peasant class, might—had he lived long enough—been able to carve his name high up on the facade of Fame's temple. As a painter he had before his acquaintance with Adele De Ivry, taken the prize in several exhibitions. He was handsome, too. They have an old portrait of him from which Eldie was to have made a new one, had her health been spared to her."

"Then, I suppose, it is from her father that Eldie gets her gift of being able to spread colors upon canvas. And he died young, did he—and left his widow and her babes for Mr. Janneaux to support?" asked Mrs. Babbit.

"The wife died first, and in six months he followed. That was out in Canada. Eldie was but three years old and Camille one, at the time of his demise. Then they came to the States, settling somewhere above St. Cloud, where they staid until they came into this neighborhood, twelve years ago."

"Bless me," said Mrs. Babbit, "how the advent of her grandfather will upset all of the ugly talk about the two girls having Indian blood in them, won't it? Now, if he came from Canada, why, even his riches and position might not save him from the imputation, as we all of us know that some of the early French settlers in those parts were apt to have squaw wives; but coming as he does, direct from the old country, where the red man is not, why, the spigot is turned on the barrel at once."

Several laughed at her odd figure.

"Who ever started such a report?" asked Mrs. Clipper.

No one could tell exactly, but it was thought that it was merely because of their rather dark complexion, coupled with a fancied peculiarity of feature, and that they passed as Canadian French.

Mrs. Babbit said that in her opinion the Janneaux never heard of the talk, but was certain that it had injured them in the community. "People will, you know," she added, "take a note of these things, socially."

Mrs. Finch was sure that they did know of it. "Eldie spoke to my Elise once about it as they were on their way to school, and said that she knew her father and mother to be of pure French extraction; also, that her mother was of good family, but as they were elopers from their native land, all trace of her people there had been lost, and there was nothing left among their early effects save the old painting from which she had made the one sold to Madame Du Boise. Therefore, she could substantiate nothing. I believe, too, from what I have heard from another source, that to this scandalizing report as to her blood, she partly laid her desertion by Lennox."

"I do not believe that," said Mrs. Fairchild. "It was all on account of that unprincipled woman, Henrietta Dudley. Had Lennox never have met her it might have been different with Eldie. But perhaps she thinks as you have said, and this thought would, in one so sensitively organized as she is, go a long way toward bringing on her decline."

Mrs. Jones until now had been a silent listener. For the first time she spoke.

"Eldie Janneaux was much worse yesterday when her sister was down to the store. She said that her grandfather had called two physicians, but that nothing could be done to save her life. A week at the farthest is the longest they expect her to last."

A good many of the party looked at the speaker in surprise. None of them had thought her so near to death's door as that, and some of them had been quite negligent in their attendance upon her as a person placed upon the sick list among them.

Therefore, some of them, at a suggestion made by Mrs. Clipper, volunteered to visit her the next day at a given hour, from the place they now were.

Just then the men came in from a back appartment, where they had been enjoying a chat and a smoke among themselves. Dinner was announced, and while it was being dispatched, Mr. Fairchild told them the news, which he had heard on his way there a half hour ago.

It was, that Charles Lennox had arrived home on a visit for a month or so, and that he was spending the most of his time at the Janneaux house. Indeed, it was surmised that the failing health of Eldie had something to do with his homecoming.

The next afternoon was a fine one, as several of the party, including Mrs. Clipper, went to see the girl whose demise was nearer than they had anticipated.

That morning there had been a change for the worse, and from that she rapidly approached her end.

About her bed had been no special prayers or religious obsequies. "Formulas of the Church," as old Mr. Janneaux called them.

He, although a Frenchman, was like Monsieur De Ivry, of the Protestant faith, and had adopted for his creed the broad one of Universalism.

His niece had been tutored under the same doctrine, and therefore her laying aside this life and the taking up of another was to be done with the assurance that it was but a change as harmonious as are all of God's laws, also without the least doubt that it was for the better.

With this confidence in the loving disposal of her life to come, her spirit was slowly ebbing out into the vast sea of eternity!

The women who came in were shocked to see

her altered appearance, and so far spent was she as to not be able to speak to them, although seemingly in a state of recognition toward them. They stayed by her until the supreme moment was over.

By the side of her sat her aunt, wetting her lips with some cordial, while her uncle held one of her wasted hands.

John Desmond was there.

He sat at the foot of the bed as if intent upon watching the last movement of the soul upon the features of the woman he loved dearer than life.

Near to him sat Lennox, his head bowed upon his hand, as if in solemn thought. All of the past was flitting through his mind as he so sat, with the eyes of the dying girl fixed steadily upon him; and in his inmost breast he, perhaps, found some germs of love, mingled with his acknowledged pity for this young creature whom he knew to be good and pure, in comparison with the false siren who had beguiled him with her charms.

John watched the fixity of her gaze with a jealous pang.

For a half hour a death-like stillness reigned in the room, broken only by the sobs of Camille, who knelt by the side of her grandfather's chair, as his great white hand rested lovingly upon her dark hair.

Then with their parting light still resting upon the object of her love, her orbs closed and the long wavering lamp of life went out to this world, just as the sun was sinking to rest in a nimbus of gold beyond the distant line of the horizon, flushing the sky with a blaze of transcendent glory! There was a pause of several minutes before any one moved or spoke.

Silent prayer was ascending from the little assembly, along with the liberated spirit to its height beyond the stars.

At the time of dissolution a noise had been heard in an adjoining room as if something had fallen. Now some of the women went in to see what it was and found the unfinished picture of the dead girl, her "Sunset Clouds," fallen over, along with the easel, as if struck by an unseen hand!

Was it mere accident, caused by some natural cause to them unknown? or was it the mysterious movement of some occult force to which the Avonic bard refers when he speaks of the "Things that we dream not of in our philosophy?"

One week after, Monsieur De Ivry, with his granddaughter, Camille, and his serving-man started for France, where the girl will be invested with all the rights to which by birth she is entitled.

THE END.

Problems Old and New.

PROBLEMS OLD AND NEW.

In the Spring of 1877, occurred the culmination of the terrible financial distress which had been settling upon many of the eastern states for several years.

Some places, indeed, most of them, have, outside of their principal business, still minor ones upon which to depend in case of a depression in the first, but this was not the case in the manufacturing centers of Pennsylvania; so in consequence of an almost total want of demand for iron—their one commodity—the suffering was great.

The proprietors had, for the sake of giving employment to their men, kept their works going until they could not, without utter ruin to themselves, proceed further.

The immense mills with their blast furnaces had lain, with the exception of an occasional short spell, in an idleness so deep that the machinery was becoming rusted through disuse, and immense piles of rails were laying about awaiting transportation when it should come.

Great fortunes were tied up in these works.

In reality nearly all of the money of the place was invested therein.

For this reason the seemingly paradoxical condition was of people who were at least nominally rich yet not able to procure the necessaries of life. Grand houses of handsome furnishing stood them but little in hand now, as they could not even mortgage what was a drug in the market. No one cared to be burdened with that which could be neither sold nor rented, and when, as if by some • irony of fate or malignity of those in power, certain improvements were set on foot in the country, so increasing the rate of taxation at this inopportune time.

There were two leading causes for this depreciation of property, the first being that of the general distress which drove people away to more prosperous regions, the second, the fact of their being mostly held by the local loan associations.

They had been built five or six years before, at a time when money was plenty and no clouds to obscure the horizon of prosperity, and at a time when the building and loan associations took their initial among them.

These were to them a new thing, imported from other parts of the country or from England, and in the hands of some monied men who wished a heavy rate of interest for their surplus cash, it was made to appear to the workingman, who in the old way used to plod along through many years in order to pay for a home, as a much easier way of obtaining one.

The affair once fairly set in motion drove people fairly out of their wits, all but a few who preferred not to trust to the new venture but to invest their hard earned dollars in the more certain way of their fathers before them. These were called old fogies by the more progressive.

Farming was the only safe calling in those woeful days, inasmuch as the man of the soil could live at least until better times should come, that is, providing that he had no encumbrances on his place, and even then would be better able to weather the storm than the man whose all was tied up in stocks, of which the shrinking value might make of the rich man of today a beggar on the morrow.

The fine buildings had been put up on all sides, borrowed by shareholders at enormous rates of interest, for as the founders had been smart enough to get the corporation fixed outside of the law against usury they, as a matter of course, could charge at their will.

People forgot all about their financial standing and the general fitness of things, so that the day laborer was induced to build for himself a residence as fine and as convenient as had the man of wealth been content with in former times. All were great folks in appearance.

The world-renowned centennial memorial of the nation's independence had been held the fall previous, drawing to it many people from different parts, some of them intent upon turning some honestly acquired pennies into their empty purses if possible, as boarding-house proprietors, restaurant keepers, shopmen, or anything appropriate to the demands of the occasion.

These, when the fair was over, found themselves so little remunerated by their venture that not a few were unable to get back to their home, except as the kindness of some more affluent friend would send them a means of railway travel, or lacking in such friend was compelled to walk the distance, hundreds of miles, perhaps, and to make affairs still worse the authorities of different cities passed laws to expel from their limits all persons found wandering about in an unemployed state, even stipulating in addition to use the railroad magnates, or officials, to carry off their surplus population into the country. By this means these people were dropped in squads all along the line, a burden to the farmers and villagers, and a prolific source for the increase of crime of all sorts, and was one of the causes which have brought about the great army of workless men known as tramps.

Then came the great strike, originated by the railroad engineers, whence it spread into all departments of labor, its greatest force concentrating in populous Pennsylvania.

These were sad days for the old Keystone state, she who in times past had been among the most prosperous of the Union, was now so racked that many of her strong men reeled in the giddiness of despair, while among the weak, blank want had brought its attendent evils of crime, insanity and suicide.

Bread! bread! was the cry in once happy and thriving America!

The riot at Pittsburg occurred, wherein the maddened mob destroyed in a few hours a million of property. Railways were demolished, trains of cars turned bodily off their track, until the state troops were called upon to quell the fury by warlike methods, many of the soldiers, in sympathy with the people, refusing to act, thus doing poor service to the government.

Telegraph communication was cut off from place to place in order to prevent news of the disturbance from spreading, but it was too late.

In the city of Scranton so great was the trouble that the Governor of the State went to them as an advisor along with the soldiers. His advice was, in addressing a body of mine proprietors, "Give to these people a sufficiency of provisions for themselves and families, otherwise I shall withdraw from your borders the aid of the military and leave you to the mercy of the starving!"

At another time, in an address, he said, "The masses are becoming enlightened and this is the effect."

His words implied that the days of vassalege are over, and though the dream of the socialist must remain but a dream, yet in the future Democracy must not be choked into a mere sound of mockery, but that its spirit must be acknowledged in the universal sentiment which will accord, at all times, a means of life to all men.

Freedom! equal rights to all!

These were the watchwords under which, as American citizens they had been fostered, but what meaning had they now to these starving people. The real sentiment of some who might have relieved their suffering was: Live upon air if you can, otherwise die of destitution or destroy yourself in your grief.

One newspaper advocated the shooting of beggars in the streets of New York, with as little ceremony as was allowed to unlicensed dogs, and at another time rejoiced in flaming headlines over the immense number of sheriff's sales!

No wonder that the suffering people were exasperated beyond endurance.

These conditions furnished a fit season for a general grab by the greedy and unscrupulous who were determined to enlarge their possessions at all hazards.

True it was that in the case of the building associations, all were considered as members of a firm united for mutual benefit, but the reciprocity continued only so long as all was flourishing, and when money ceased to flow in there was a turn in the tide of brotherly feeling, so that the weaker part of the fraternity were, after a figure, like as many fish stranded upon the shore with a net in the hands of the stronger part tightly drawn about them. They might flounder and writhe in their agony, but there was no mercy.

In the town of D—— a number of workless men set forth their wretched condition and their utter inability to keep up the monthly dues, praying for a suspension of business transactions at the time, and that they be permitted to remain in their

homes until a period when they might resume
payments.

The petition was unheeded among the non-bor-
rowers, who were not thus to be balked in their
schemes of a vast profit from their money. "Our
cash returned with its great interest or else the
property is ours," was the cry; said properties, in
varying degrees, representing much more in value
than the original purchase money, this fact increasing the temptation for seizure.

Many had owned the ground upon which the
building was set, but all was given as security to
the lenders, while others had put extra additions
to their homes and much labor and expense upon
the surroundings, causing them to be a very
representation of thrift.

Executions proceeded in due order as one delinquent after another appeared upon the list, so that
the sheriff with his notice, and the constable with
his officers were the bug-bears which, either in
fact or in expectation, kept the men in a state of
sullen despair and the women in one of terror.
These officials, with lawyers and tax collectors,
were the only busy people to be found, but in time
the greedy mortgagors saw their mistake.

One entire suburb—a village in itself—passed
into their hands, and the consequence was that as
many of the inhabitants who could get means
sufficient, left for the west or south, and as ten-
ants could not be found for the vacated buildings,
upon which insurance was hard to pay, the place
fell into general ruin, leaving the owners with a

load of valueless property upon their hands, of which they were willing to rid themselves at any cost.

At the contingent manufacturing town the ensign of distress was also raised and confusion most dire prevailed.

The wild mob, maddened by the pangs of hunger, took possession of the only place of military furnishment that the place afforded, armed themselves with rifles and revolvers, together with a store of ammunition, and thus fortified paraded the streets in an attitude of threatening until a meeting of leading citizens was called who demanded a cause for the rash movement of these work-people, whose real condition was kept from them by the fact that their place of residence was set apart from the more aristocratic portions of the place.

Then one after another told their condition of almost universal sameness, the most startling and appalling feature being a statement by some that themselves and children had for several days had no nourishment but that which was afforded by mountain tea!

Ignorant! thriftless! the slums!

Perhaps they were or perhaps they were not, but all events they yet belonged to the great brotherhood of mankind, and so were worthy of of consideration, and they are not at all times to blame for coming into a state of destitution, especially during a time of financial stringency; as they belong, many of them to a class who are poor, not so much from laziness as from a deficiency in that selfish greed so necessary in persons of their class who wish to get anything beyond their daily needs, and even in the case of the spendthrift, his expenditures only pass into the hands of those more fitted to get and to keep.

These people were easily satisfied.

With a spirit placable enough to merit the phrase applied their compeers of old in France, "Bonne Homme Jacques," they accepted the meager wages which would accrue from a labor of two days out of each week at one dollar and a half per day upon the streets. This is to the head of a family.

To a strong lover of life it was better than death, as it might by judicious expenditure keep body and soul together.

These wretched conditions were new ones in America, new to her people, although some of them had read of like times in England when Jack Cada and Wat Tyler at different times led their hungry followers to London; also the same in pleasure-loving, impetuous, unstable France, at the time of Marcel, Robespierre, Danton and others, and shuddered to think that in their own land affairs should approach anything like those bygone days.

What is the cure for such national griefs? it may be asked.

Enlightment for all is the only remedy. Not only in the book-learning of our schools, but also, of each sex among all classes, in the workings of

both corporation and state laws, and in a stronger
sense of Christian duty, one to another, than has
as yet dawned upon our world's horizon despite
all of the money spent in the erection of churches.
To these last, and to parents, belong much of the
solving of the labor problem, but parents cannot
properly assist the schools in training their children unless they be first informed themselves.
Therefore read for enlightment's sake.

The household wherein no good reading is done
is a poor one, though it possess millions in
money!

It was through the cause of this struggle that
the banking house of Isaacs & Company collapsed,
causing the beautiful and accomplished daughter of the senior member to retire from a world of
fashion to one of poverty and of meditation,
where came to her revelations from the invisible
world, wrought by invisible powers, and which fell
upon her with astounding surprise, inasmuch as
in the religious training which she had received
among her people of the synagogue of Israel, no
mention had been made of such occult manifesta-
tions, neither among the Christian sects had she
ever heard anything of the kind; and except
some vague rumors which had reached her ears
from spiritual circles as to the doctrines of a
mystic world, all was darkness to her until, by an
intent searching among the prophetic writings
the mystery was made clear to her understanding,
according to Jewish conception, but was the
mysterious force the same Supreme Fatherhood ˙

working through the phenomena of miracles to all people and throughout all times according to their power of reception and seeking as media such as had overcome sufficiently to reconcile the natural with the spiritual law?

Her strongly reasoning mind told her that this solution must be the right one, only it had been a severe task for her intellectual and moral nature to work it out all unaided by superior lights; also, she believed it possible for some to be able, through interior development, to receive and yet not be able through search to hear the divine voice, and to such how dire might be the consequences!

THE END.

www.ingramcontent.com/pod-product-compliance
Lightning Source LLC
Chambersburg PA
CBHW030345270326
41926CB00009B/965